Let's Get Cooking

Skinny
Slow Cooking

Over **100** hearty recipes

igloobooks

igloobooks

Published in 2017
by Igloo Books Ltd
Cottage Farm
Sywell
NN6 0BJ
www.igloobooks.com

Designed by Nicholas Gage
Edited by Jasmin Peppiatt

All imagery: © iStock / Getty Images

REX001 0617
2 4 6 8 10 9 7 5 3 1
ISBN 978-1-78670-920-2

Printed and manufactured in China

Contents

Meat and Fish 6

Vegetables, Herbs and More 36

Soups 60

Desserts 72

Meat and Fish

SERVES: **2** | PREP TIME: **10 MINS** | COOKING TIME: **3 HOURS 5 MINS**

Waterbath Lamb Chops

4 lamb chops
2 sprigs rosemary, plus extra to garnish
2 cloves of garlic, unpeeled
  and squashed
2 tbsp olive oil
6 mushrooms, halved

1. Season the lamb chops with salt and pepper then put them in a zip-lock freezer bag with the rosemary, garlic and oil. Seal the bags, excluding as much air as possible.
2. Put the bag in a slow cooker and weigh it down with a plate.
3. Add enough water to cover the lamb by 5 cm (2 in) and set the temperature to low.
4. Cook the lamb for 3 hours.
5. Use a thermometer to ensure the water temperature doesn't exceed 60°C (140F) and turn off the slow cooker if needed.
6. Remove the lamb from the bag and blot dry with kitchen paper.
7. Heat a griddle pan until smoking hot, then griddle the lamb and mushrooms for 2 minutes on each side to sear.
8. Serve immediately, garnished with extra rosemary.

Creamy Chicken with Peas

2 tbsp olive oil
4 chicken thighs, on the bone
3 shallots, finely chopped
225 g / 8 oz / 3 cups button
  mushrooms, sliced
2 rashers bacon, chopped
2 cloves of garlic, finely chopped
2 tbsp Pernod
500 ml / 17 ½ fl. oz / 2 cups chicken stock
150 g / 5 ½ oz / 1 cup frozen peas, defrosted
75 ml / 1 ¾ fl. oz / ⅓ cup Greek yogurt

1. Heat the oil in a frying pan. Season the chicken with salt and pepper, then sear the skin side until golden brown. Set aside.
2. Add the shallots, mushrooms, bacon and garlic to the pan and sauté for 10 minutes or until lightly coloured. Deglaze the pan with the Pernod, then scrape the mixture into a slow cooker.
3. Arrange the chicken on top, skin side up, then cover and cook on medium for 4 hours
4. Stir the peas into the sauce and cook for another 30 minutes.
5. Stir the yogurt into the sauce just before serving to prevent it from splitting, then season to taste with salt and pepper.

Risotto Baked Pumpkins

1 litre / 1 pint 15 fl. oz / 4 cups
  vegetable stock
2 tbsp olive oil
1 onion, finely chopped
1 carrot, finely chopped
2 cloves of garlic, crushed
4 thick rashers bacon, chopped
150 g / 5 ½ oz / ¾ cup risotto rice
50 g / 1 ¾ oz / ½ cup Parmesan, finely grated
2 small culinary pumpkins, tops sliced off
  and seeds removed

1. Heat the stock in a saucepan and keep it just below simmering point.
2. Heat the olive oil in a sauté pan and gently fry the onion and carrot for 5 minutes without colouring. Add the garlic and bacon and cook for 5 more minutes or until golden, then stir in the rice.
3. When it is well coated with the oil, add half of the stock and cook for 8 minutes, stirring occasionally. Stir in the rest of the stock and cook for 5 minutes, then stir in the Parmesan.
4. Arrange the pumpkins side by side in a large oval slow cooker and fill with the par-cooked risotto, then put the tops back on.
5. Pour enough boiling water into the slow cooker to come half way up the sides of the pumpkins, then cover and cook on high for 5 hours or until a skewer slides easily into the pumpkins.

Cottage Pie

2 tbsp olive oil
1 onion, finely chopped
2 cloves of garlic, crushed
1 tbsp fresh thyme, stalks removed,
  plus extra to garnish
450 g / 1 lb / 2 cups minced beef
400 g / 14 oz / 1 ¾ cups canned
  tomatoes, chopped
200 ml / 7 fl. oz / ¾ cup beef stock

FOR THE TOPPING
450 g / 1 lb floury potatoes, peeled
  and cubed
150 ml / 5 ½ fl. oz / ⅔ cup skimmed milk
50 g / 1 ¾ oz / ½ cup reduced fat
  Cheddar, grated

1. Heat the oil in a large frying pan and fry the onion for 10 minutes, stirring occasionally. Add the garlic and thyme and cook for 2 minutes, then add the mince.
2. Fry the mince until it starts to brown then scrape the mixture into a slow cooker and add the tomatoes and stock.
3. Cover the slow cooker and cook on medium for 5 hours.
4. Near the end of the cooking time, cook the potatoes in water for 12 minutes then drain well. Return the potatoes to the saucepan. Add the milk. Mash until smooth.
5. Transfer the cooked mince to a serving dish and top with mashed potatoes and cheese. Cook under a hot grill for a few minutes to brown the top, then serve, garnished with thyme.

Braised Beef
with Oyster Sauce

2 tbsp sunflower oil
450 g / 1 lb / 3 cups shin of beef, cut into
  large chunks
3 cloves of garlic, peeled and squashed
30 g / 1 oz piece of fresh root
  ginger, sliced
4 spring onions (scallions), green part
  sliced, the rest bruised
75 ml / 2 ½ fl. oz / ⅓ cup shaoxing rice wine
75 ml / 2 ½ fl. oz / ⅓ cup oyster sauce
2 tbsp dark soy sauce
steamed rice, to serve
1 handful coriander (cilantro) leaves

1. Heat the oil in a frying pan and sear the beef on all sides. Transfer the beef to a slow cooker and add the garlic, ginger, spring onion whites, rice wine, oyster sauce and soy sauce.
2. Add enough cold water to just cover the beef, then cover and cook on low for 6 hours.
3. Strain the cooking liquor into a wide saucepan and reduce over a high heat until just thick enough to coat the beef.
4. Serve the beef on a bed of steamed rice with the sauce spooned over. Garnish with coriander leaves and spring onion greens.

SERVES: **4** | PREP TIME: **25 MINS** | COOKING TIME: **8 HOURS**

Rich Braised Lamb Shanks

2 tbsp olive oil
1 onion, quartered and sliced
2 cloves of garlic, finely chopped
4 lamb shanks
2 tbsp plain (all-purpose) flour
4 carrots, peeled and cut into batons
400 ml / 14 fl. oz / 1 ⅔ cups port
400 ml / 14 fl. oz / 1 ⅔ cups lamb or beef stock
1 sprig of rosemary

1. Heat the oil in a frying pan and fry the onion and garlic for 10 minutes or until soft and golden. Season with salt and pepper, then tip it into a slow cooker.
2. Dust the lamb shanks with flour, then sear them all over in the frying pan.
   Sit the lamb on top of the onions and surround with the carrots.
3. Pour the port into the frying pan and boil for 5 minutes, then pour it into the slow cooker with the stock and rosemary.
4. Cook on high for 8 hours or until the lamb is tender and the sauce is thick and rich.
   Taste and adjust the seasoning before serving.

MAKES: 6 | **PREP TIME: 45 MINS** | **COOKING TIME: 2 HOURS 50 MINS**

Mini Quiches

2 tbsp olive oil
1 small onion, finely chopped
2 thick rashers smoked streaky
  bacon, chopped
1 clove of garlic, finely chopped
3 large eggs
200 ml / 7 fl. oz / ¾ cup skimmed milk
100 g / 3 ½ oz / 1 cup reduced fat
  Cheddar, grated

FOR THE PASTRY
100 g / 3 ½ oz / ½ cup reduced fat
  baking spread, cubed
200 g / 7 oz / 1 ⅓ cups plain
  (all purpose) flour
1 large egg, beaten

1. To make the pastry, rub the baking spread into the flour until the mixture resembles fine breadcrumbs.
2. Stir in enough cold water to bring the pastry together into a pliable dough and chill for 30 minutes.
3. Meanwhile, heat the oil in a frying pan and fry the onion for 5 minutes. Add the bacon and garlic and cook for another 5 minutes.
4. Gently whisk the eggs with the milk until smoothly combined then stir in the bacon mixture and two thirds of the cheese. Season generously with salt and pepper.
5. Roll out the pastry on a floured surface and cut out six circles with a cookie cutter. Transfer the pastry circles to a six-hole cupcake tin that will fit inside your slow cooker.
6. Cover the slow cooker with a clean tea towel, then put on the lid. Cook on high for 1 hour.
7. Pour the filling into the pastry cases and sprinkle with the rest of the cheese, then cover with the tea towel and lid and cook on low for 1 hour 30 minutes.

SERVES: **4** | PREP TIME: **10 MINS** | COOKING TIME: **3 HOURS**

Sausage and Lentil Stew

2 tbsp olive oil
16 small sausages
1 onion, sliced
1 stick celery, sliced
1 red pepper, deseeded and diced
2 cloves of garlic, sliced
200 g / 7 oz / 1 cup green lentils
400 g / 14 oz / 2 cups canned tomatoes, chopped
1 bay leaf
1 large handful flat leaf parsley

1. Heat the oil in a large frying pan and brown the sausages all over.
2. Transfer to a slow cooker and stir in the rest of the ingredients, except for the parsley. Fill up the tomato can with water and stir it in.
3. Cover and cook on medium for 3 hours.
4. Taste the stew for seasoning and adjust with salt and pepper, then discard the bay leaf and stir in the parsley.
5. Ladle into warm bowls and serve.

SERVES: 4 | PREP TIME: 45 MINS | COOKING TIME: 3 HOURS

Steak and Swede Slice

225 g / 8 oz / 1 ½ cups plain (all-purpose) flour

110 g / 4 oz / ½ cup reduced fat baking spread, cubed and chilled

225 g / 8 oz / 1 ½ cups beef skirt, cut into 1 cm (⅓ in) cubes

1 small onion, finely chopped

150 g / 5 ½ oz / 1 ¼ cups swede, peeled and grated

150 g / 5 ½ oz / 1 ¼ cups potato, peeled and grated

1. Reserve 1 tablespoon of flour then rub the baking spread into the rest until the mixture resembles fine breadcrumbs. Stir in just enough cold water to bring the pastry together into a pliable dough, then chill for 30 minutes.

2. Roll out the pastry to match the length and twice the width of a large oval slow cooker.

3. Toss the beef with the onion, swede, potato and reserved tablespoon of flour and season generously with salt and pepper. Spread the mixture over one half of the pastry, then fold it other and crimp tightly to seal.

4. Line the slow cooker with a large sheet of greaseproof paper and lower in the steak slice. Cover and cook on high for 1 hour 30 minutes.

5. Carefully remove the steak slice using the greaseproof paper and turn it over. Lower it back into the slow cooker, then cover and cook for 1 hour 30 minutes or until the pastry is cooked through.

6. Cut the steak slice into quarters and serve hot or at room temperature.

SERVES: 4 | PREP TIME: 5 MINS | COOKING TIME: 6 HOURS

Spanish Chicken Bake

200 g / 7 oz / 1 cup canned
   tomatoes, chopped
1 clove of garlic, crushed
½ tsp smoked paprika
1 yellow pepper, deseeded and sliced
150 g / 5 ½ oz / 1 cup cherry
   tomatoes, halved
1 handful black olives
4 chicken drumsticks
2 tbsp sundried tomato paste
a few sprigs of rosemary
2 tbsp olive oil

1. Tip the canned tomatoes into a
   small slow cooker and stir in the
   garlic, paprika and ½ a teaspoon
   of salt. Arrange the peppers,
   cherry tomatoes and olives on top.
2. Spread the chicken drumsticks with
   the sundried tomato paste and lay
   them on top, then scatter over the
   rosemary and drizzle with oil.
3. Cover and cook on medium for
   6 hours or until the chicken is
   very tender.
4. Season to taste with salt and pepper
   before serving.

Paella

1 litre / 1 pint 15 fl. oz / 4 cups fish stock
a pinch of saffron
50 ml / 1 ¾ fl. oz / ¼ cup olive oil
1 onion, finely chopped
1 red pepper, finely chopped
2 cloves of garlic, crushed
200 g / 7 oz / 1 cup paella rice
100 ml / 3 ½ fl. oz / ½ cup dry sherry
8 raw king prawns
8 green-lip mussels
8 clams
lemon wedges, to serve

1. Heat the stock in a saucepan with the saffron, but don't let it boil.
2. Heat the olive oil in a frying pan and fry the onion and peppers over a low heat for 15 minutes, stirring occasionally. Add the garlic and cook for 2 minutes, then add the rice and stir over a low heat for 3 minutes to toast it slightly. Add the sherry and simmer until almost completely evaporated.
3. Scrape the contents of the pan into a slow cooker and add the hot stock. Season with salt and pepper and stir well, then cover and cook on high for 1 hour 45 minutes.
4. Press the prawns, mussels and clams down into the rice, then cover and cook for another 15 minutes or until the shells have opened and the prawns have turned pink.
5. The paella can be served straight from the slow cooker. Alternatively, transfer it to a paella pan and brown for a few minutes under a hot grill. Serve with lemon wedges.

Ragu for Pasta

2 tbsp olive oil
1 onion, finely chopped
1 large carrot, diced
1 stick celery, diced
1 tbsp fresh thyme leaves
4 cloves of garlic, finely chopped
450 g / 1 lb / 3 cups shin of beef, cubed
2 tbsp concentrated tomato puree
200 ml / 7 fl. oz / ¾ cup red wine
400 ml / 14 fl. oz / 1 ½ cups beef stock
2 tbsp flat leaf parsley, chopped
tagliatelle to serve

1. Heat the oil in a large frying pan and fry the onion, carrot, celery and thyme for 10 minutes, stirring occasionally. Add the garlic and beef and fry until the meat starts to brown then stir in the tomato puree.
2. Pour in the wine and boil rapidly for 2 minutes, then scrape everything into a slow cooker with the beef stock.
3. Cover the slow cooker and cook on medium for 5 hours, then season with salt and pepper to taste. The meat should be falling apart into shreds by this time.
4. Stir in the parsley and serve with freshly cooked tagliatelle.

SERVES: **4** | PREP TIME: **20 MINS** | COOKING TIME: **3 HOURS**

Cod, Broccoli and Potato Gratin

3 medium potatoes, peeled and cut into chunks
2 tbsp reduced fat baking spread
2 tbsp plain (all-purpose) flour
600 ml / 1 pint / 2 ½ cups skimmed milk
1 tbsp Dijon mustard
100 g / 3 ½ oz / 1 cup reduced fat Cheddar, grated
1 small broccoli, broken into florets
250 g / 9 oz / 1 ⅔ cups skinless boneless cod, cut into large chunks

1. Boil the potatoes in salted water for 10 minutes, then drain well.
2. Meanwhile, put the baking spread, flour and milk in a saucepan.
3. Stir over a medium heat until it bubbles and thickens, then stir in the cheddar. Season with salt and pepper to taste.
4. Mix the potatoes with the broccoli and cod in a flan dish that will fit snugly inside your slow cooker and top with the sauce.
5. Make a cross from strips of foil inside the slow cooker to help you remove the flan dish, then lower it in. Cover and cook on medium for 3 hours or until the broccoli is tender to the point of a knife.
6. Remove the flan dish from the slow cooker and brown the top under a hot grill for a few minutes before serving.

SERVES: 6 | PREP TIME: 15 MINS | COOKING TIME: 7 HOURS

Chorizo and Butterbean Stew

300 g / 10 ½ oz / 2 cups dried
    butterbeans, soaked overnight
4 cooking chorizo, sliced
1 onion, chopped
2 small carrots, sliced
1 stick celery, sliced
2 cloves of garlic, sliced
1 bay leaf
150 g / 5 ½ oz / 1 cup sundried tomatoes
750 ml / 1 pint 5 ½ fl. oz / 3 cups
    chicken stock

TO SERVE
250 g / 9 oz / 2 balls mozzarella, torn into
    small chunks
1 small bunch flat leaf parsley, chopped
1 small bunch dill, chopped

1. Drain the beans of their soaking water, then tip them into a saucepan, cover with cold water and bring to the boil. Cook for 10 minutes then drain well.

2. Meanwhile, cook the chorizo slices in a hot frying pan until coloured on both sides.

3. Tip the beans and chorizo into a slow cooker and stir in the rest of the ingredients. Cover and cook on medium for 7 hours or until the beans are tender. Season to taste with salt and pepper.

4. Divide the stew between six warm bowls and arrange the mozzarella, parsley and dill on top.

Chicken and Vegetable Broth

3 skinless chicken breasts, cut into chunks
2 carrots, peeled and crinkle cut
2 sticks celery, sliced
3 medium potatoes, peeled and diced
1 head broccoli, broken into florets
1 onion, finely chopped
1 litre / 1 pint 15 fl. oz / 4 cups
  chicken stock
150 g / 5 ½ oz / 1 cup peas,
  defrosted if frozen

1. Mix all of the ingredients except for the peas in a slow cooker and season with salt and pepper.
2. Cover and cook on medium for 2 hours or until the vegetables are tender and the chicken is cooked.
3. Turn off the heat, then add the peas, cover and leave to stand for 5 minutes.
4. Ladle into four bowls and serve immediately.

Garlic Baked Chicken

1 chicken, jointed into 12 pieces
1 bulb of garlic, separated into cloves
1 lemon, juiced
2 tbsp Stevia
75 ml / 2 ½ fl. oz / ⅓ cup reduced sodium
  soy sauce

1. Mix all of the ingredients together in a slow cooker and season with black pepper.
2. Cover and cook on medium for 3 hours, stirring once an hour.
3. Transfer everything to a baking dish and brown under a hot grill for a few minutes to finish.

SERVES: 4 | PREP TIME: 30 MINS | COOKING TIME: 2 HOURS

Lamb Chops with Tomato Sauce

2 tbsp olive oil
16 small lamb chops
100 ml / 3 ½ fl. oz / ½ cup dry white wine
1 onion, finely chopped
2 cloves of garlic, crushed
400 ml / 7 fl. oz / 1 ⅔ cups tomato passata
2 tsp dried mint
400 g / 14 oz linguini

1. Heat the oil in a frying pan and sear the lamb chops on both sides.
2. Transfer the lamb to a slow cooker and add the wine to the frying pan. Simmer for 2 minutes, then pour into the slow cooker and add the onion, garlic and passata.
3. Cover and cook on high for 2 hours.
4. Boil the linguini in salted water according to the packet instructions or until al dente. Drain well.
5. While the pasta is cooking, remove the lamb from the slow cooker and scrape most of the sauce back into the pot. Sprinkle the lamb with dried mint and cook under a hot grill for a few minutes on each side to caramelise the sauce.
6. Stir the linguini into the tomato sauce and serve with the lamb chops.

Lamb Hotpot

1 kg / 2 lb 3 ½ oz / 7 cups boneless lamb
  neck, cubed
3 lamb kidneys, trimmed and quartered
2 tbsp olive oil
1 onion, chopped
2 carrots, peeled and cut into chunks
2 sticks celery, cut into chunks
6 sprigs fresh thyme
1 tbsp plain (all-purpose) flour
800 ml / 1 pint 7 fl. oz / 3 ¼ cups lamb
  or chicken stock
1 kg / 2 lb 3 ½ oz potatoes

1. Preheat the oven to 160°C (140° fan) / 325F / gas 3.
2. Blot the lamb and kidneys with kitchen paper to ensure they are completely dry
   then season with salt and pepper. Heat the oil in a frying pan over a high heat then
   sear the lamb and kidneys in batches until browned all over.
3. Remove the meat from the pan, lower the heat a little and add the onions,
   carrots, celery and thyme. Cook for 10 minutes, stirring occasionally.
4. Increase the heat and stir in the flour then incorporate the stock and bring to a
   simmer. Arrange the lamb and kidneys in a casserole dish and pour over the
   stock and vegetables.
5. Slice the potatoes 5 mm (¼ in) thick with a sharp knife or mandolin and arrange
   them on top of the lamb.
6. Cover the dish tightly with foil or a lid. Bake for 2 hours 30 minutes, then remove
   the foil and bake for another 30 minutes to colour the top.

Chicken Pie Filling

4 chicken leg quarters
1 carrot, cut into chunks
1 stick celery, cut into chunks
1 leek, cut into chunks
2 tsp cornflour (corn starch)
1 tsp Dijon mustard
150 ml / 5 ½ fl. oz / ⅔ cup 0 per cent
  fat Greek yogurt
1 courgette (zucchini), chopped

FOR THE PASTRY
200 g / 7 oz / 1 cup reduced fat baking
  spread, cubed and chilled
400 g / 14 oz / 2 ⅔ cups plain
  (all purpose) flour
1 egg, beaten

1. Put the chicken, carrot, celery and leek in a slow cooker and add enough water to
   cover. Cover and cook on medium for 4 hours.
2. Strain and reserve the stock. Discard the vegetables, chicken skin and bones then
   shred the chicken into pieces. Stir the cornflour and mustard into the yogurt then
   stir in the chicken and enough of the stock to make a thin sauce. Leave to cool.
3. While the filling is cooking, rub the butter into the flour until the mixture resembles
   breadcrumbs. Stir in water to bring the pastry into a dough. Chill for 30 minutes.
4. Preheat the oven to 200°C (180° fan) / 400F / gas 6. Roll out ⅔ of the pastry on a
   floured surface and use it to line a pie dish. Spoon in the filling then brush round
   the rim with water. Roll out the rest of the pastry and lay it over the top. Trim away
   any excess. Crimp round the edge with a fork and brush the top with beaten egg.
   Make a few steam holes on top with a sharp knife.
5. Bake the pie for 45 minutes.

SERVES: 6 | PREP TIME: 20 MINS | COOKING TIME: 6 HOURS 30 MINS

Sausage, Bean and Barley Soup

300 g / 10 ½ oz / 2 cup dried haricot beans, soaked overnight

200 g / 7 oz / 1 cup pearl barley

1 onion, finely chopped

2 cloves of garlic, chopped

2 bay leaves

4 tomatoes, chopped

6 Toulouse sausages, skinned and broken into pieces

2 large handfuls spinach, washed

2 tbsp Parmesan, finely grated

1. Drain the beans from their soaking water and put them in a large saucepan of cold water.
2. Bring to the boil and cook for 10 minutes then drain well.
3. Mix the beans with the barley, onion, garlic, bay leaves and sausages in a slow cooker. Pour over enough boiling water to cover everything by 5 cm (2 in), then cook on low for 6 hours or until the beans are tender, but still holding their shape.
4. Season to taste with salt and pepper, then stir in the spinach and cook for a further 30 minutes.
5. Ladle the soup into bowls and sprinkle with Parmesan before serving.

Lamb, Apricot and Chickpea Tagine

450 g / 1 lb / 2 cups lamb shoulder, cubed
2 tbsp olive oil
1 onion, finely chopped
1 large carrot, diced
2 cloves of garlic, finely chopped
2 tsp ras el hanout spice mix
100 g / 3 ½ oz / ¾ cup dried chickpeas
600 ml / 1 pint / 2 ½ cups lamb or vegetable stock
150 g / 5 ½ oz / 1 cup dried apricots
½ pomegranate, seeds only
2 tbsp flat leaf parsley, chopped

1. Season the lamb all over with salt and pepper. Heat the oil in a frying pan and sear the lamb on all sides, then transfer the pieces to a slow cooker.
2. Fry the onion, carrot and garlic in the frying pan for 5 minutes, then stir in the ras el hanout.
3. Scrape the mixture into the slow cooker and add the chickpeas and stock.
4. Cover and cook on medium for 6 hours, adding the apricots after 4 hours.
5. Season to taste with salt and pepper and ladle into warm bowls.
6. Garnish with pomegranate seeds and parsley.

SERVES: 6 | **PREP TIME: 10 MINS** | COOKING TIME: **3 HOURS**

Sausage and Vegetable Casserole

1 tbsp olive oil
6 good quality sausages
1 onion, finely chopped
2 sticks celery, diced
2 carrots, sliced
2 cloves of garlic, sliced
1 tsp smoked paprika
150 g / 5 ½ oz / ¾ cup green lentils
400 g / 14 oz / 2 cups canned tomatoes, chopped
1 handful coriander (cilantro) leaves

1. Heat the oil in a large frying pan and brown the sausages all over.
2. Transfer to a slow cooker and stir in the rest of the ingredients, except for the coriander. Fill up the tomato can with water and stir it in.
3. Cover and cook on medium for 3 hours.
4. Taste the stew for seasoning and adjust with salt and pepper.
5. Ladle into warm bowls and serve garnished with coriander.

Prawn and Vegetable Curry

2 tbsp Thai green curry paste
400 ml / 14 fl. oz / 1 ⅔ cups light coconut milk
200 ml / 7 fl. oz / ¾ cup fish stock
1 carrot, crinkle cut
1 small aubergine (eggplant), cubed
150 g / 5 ½ oz / 1 cup green beans, cut
  into short lengths
1 red pepper, quartered and sliced
1 courgette (zucchini), crinkle cut
1–2 tbsp fish sauce
2–3 tsp caster (superfine) sugar
300 g / 10 ½ oz / 2 cups raw king prawns,
  peeled with tails left intact
steamed rice, to serve

1. Stir the curry paste into the coconut milk in a slow cooker until dissolved then stir in the stock.
2. Add the vegetables, then cover and cook on low for 2 hours.
3. Season to taste with fish sauce and caster sugar, then stir in the prawns.
4. Cover and cook for 15 minutes, then serve immediately with steamed rice.

Cheesy Chicken Bake

1 large aubergine, thinly sliced
150 ml / 5 ½ fl. oz / ⅔ cup dry white wine
3 skinless chicken breasts, sliced
225 g / 8 oz / 1 ½ cups cherry
  tomatoes, halved
125 g / 4 ½ oz / 1 ball light
  mozzarella, grated
100 g / 3 ½ oz / 1 cup reduced fat
  Cheddar, grated
100 g / 3 ½ oz / ½ cup low fat soft cheese
1 tsp herbs de Provence
1 clove of garlic, crushed

1. Arrange the aubergine slices in a slow cooker and season with salt and pepper. Pour over the wine, then top with the chicken and tomatoes.
2. Mix the mozzarella, Cheddar, soft cheese, herbs and garlic together and dot the mixture over the top.
3. Cover and cook on medium for 3 hours or until the chicken is cooked through.
4. If you prefer, the top can be coloured under a hot grill just before serving.

Thai Fish Soup

2 tbsp Thai curry paste
400 ml / 14 fl. oz / 1 ⅔ cups light
   coconut milk
500 ml / 17 ½ fl. oz / 2 cups fish stock
4 kaffir lime leaves
2 stalks lemongrass
8 spring onions (scallions), cut into
   short lengths
2 whole sea bass, gutted and scaled
1–2 tbsp fish sauce
1-2 tsp stevia
1 lime, juiced
1 small bunch coriander (cilantro),
   roughly chopped

1. Stir the curry paste into the coconut milk in a slow cooker until dissolved then stir
   in the stock, lime leaves, lemon grass and spring onions.
2. Carefully lower in the fish so that they lie in a single layer, then cover and cook
   on low for 1 hour 30 minutes.
3. Carefully lift the fish out of the soup with a couple of fish slices and transfer to
   a plate. Remove the skin, heads and bones and carefully break the flesh into
   large chunks.
4. Season the soup to taste with fish sauce, stevia and lime juice, then return the
   fish to the pot.
5. Serve immediately, garnished with coriander.

Mini Toad in the Holes with Gravy

2 tbsp olive oil
2 onions, halved and sliced
1 tbsp balsamic vinegar
1 tbsp runny honey
1 tbsp plain (all-purpose) flour
50 ml / 1 ¾ fl. oz / ¼ cup dry Marsala
500 ml / 17 ½ fl. oz / 2 cups chicken stock
2 tbsp lard
6 good quality sausages, halved
75 g / 2 ½ oz / ½ cup plain
   (all purpose) flour
2 large eggs
100 ml / 3 ½ oz / ½ cup skimmed milk
rosemary sprigs, to garnish

1. Heat the oil in a slow cooker on high for 15 minutes. Stir in the onions, balsamic and
   honey. Cover and cook on high for 1 hour, stirring every 15 minutes.
2. Stir in the flour, then gradually incorporate the Marsala and stock. Cover and cook
   on low for 4 hours, stirring occasionally.
3. An hour before you want to serve, preheat the oven to 230°C (210°C fan) / 450F /
   gas 8. Heat 1 teaspoon of lard in a frying pan and brown the sausages all over.
4. Put a blob of lard into each hole of a 12-hole muffin tin. Put in the oven to heat.
5. Put the flour in a large jug with a pinch of salt, then whisk in the eggs and milk.
6. Take the muffin tin out of the oven, add a sausage half to each hole and divide the
   batter between them. Return the tin to the oven and bake for 35 minutes without
   opening the door. Serve the toads with onion gravy and rosemary to garnish.

Shepherd's Pie

2 tbsp olive oil
2 large onion, finely chopped
2 cloves of garlic, crushed
2 tsp fresh rosemary, finely chopped
450 g / 1 lb / 2 cups lean minced lamb
500 ml / 17 ½ fl. oz / 2 cups lamb or
  beef stock
1 tsp Worcester sauce
2 tsp redcurrant jelly
2 tsp fresh mint, finely chopped

FOR THE TOPPING
450 g / 1 lb floury potatoes,
  peeled and cubed
150 ml / 5 ½ fl. oz / ⅔ cup skimmed milk
50 g / 1 ¾ oz / ⅔ cup fresh breadcrumbs
50 g / 1 ¾ oz / ½ cup reduced fat
  Cheddar, grated

1. Heat the oil in a large frying pan and fry the onions for 10 minutes, stirring occasionally. Add the garlic and rosemary and cook for 2 minutes, then add the mince.
2. Fry the mince until it starts to brown then scrape the mixture into a slow cooker and add the stock, Worcester sauce and redcurrant jelly.
3. Cover the slow cooker and cook on medium for 5 hours.
4. Towards the end of the cooking time, cook the potatoes in salted water for 12 minutes, or until they are tender, then drain well. Return the potatoes to the saucepan and add the milk, then mash until smooth.
5. Stir the mint into the cooked mince and season to taste with salt and pepper. Transfer it to an ovenproof frying pan and top with mashed potatoes.
6. Mix the breadcrumbs with the cheese and scatter over the top, then cook under a hot grill for a few minutes or until golden brown.

Beef Stroganoff

2 tbsp olive oil
450 g / 1 lb braising steak, sliced
1 large onion, chopped
150 g / 5 ½ oz / 2 cups button
  mushrooms, sliced
1 tsp Hungarian paprika
250 ml / 9 fl. oz / 1 cup beef stock
250 ml / 9 fl. oz / 1 cup half fat soured cream
1 small bunch flat-leaf parsley, chopped
boiled rice, to serve

1. Heat half the oil in a frying pan and sear the steak slices on both sides in batches. Transfer to a slow cooker.
2. Add the rest of the oil to the pan and fry the onions over a medium heat for 10 minutes to soften. Scrape the onions into the slow cooker and add the mushrooms, paprika and stock.
3. Cover the cook on low for 4 hours.
4. Stir in the soured cream and season to taste with salt and pepper.
5. Cover and cook for 2 hours or until the beef is tender.
6. Sprinkle the stroganoff with parsley and serve with boiled rice.

SERVES: 6 | PREP TIME: 30 MINS | MARINATE: 2 HOURS | COOKING TIME: 6 HOURS

Roast Beef Rib

1 tbsp fresh rosemary, finely chopped
1 tbsp fresh thyme leaves
2 cloves of garlic, crushed
2 tbsp olive oil
1.8 kg / 4 lb rib of beef, on the bone
2 onions, sliced
250 ml / 9 fl. oz / 1 cup red wine
250 ml / 9 fl. oz / 1 cup beef stock
1 tbsp plain (all-purpose) flour, (optional)

1. Mix the rosemary, thyme and garlic and rub it all over the beef. Season all over with salt and pepper, then leave to marinate at room temperature for 2 hours.

2. Heat the oil in a large frying pan and sear the beef all over until well browned.

3. Arrange the onions in an even layer in a slow cooker and sit the beef on top. Pour in the wine and stock.

4. Cover and cook on low for 6 hours or until it reaches an internal temperature of 54°C (130F) when checked with a probe thermometer.

5. Transfer the meat to a carving board and cover with a double layer of foil. Leave to rest for 15 minutes.

6. Meanwhile, strain the cooking liquor into a saucepan and bring to the boil. Reduce the liquid until it tastes suitably flavoursome. It can then be thickened by whisking in a little flour if you prefer.

7. Carve the beef into thick slices and serve the gravy on the side.

SERVES: **6** | PREP TIME: **5 MINS** | COOKING TIME: **3 HOURS**

Peppers Stuffed
with Prawns and Aubergines

1 red onion, finely chopped
150 ml / 5 ½ fl. oz / ⅔ cup dry white wine
3 red peppers, halved and deseeded
150 g / 5 ½ oz / 1 cup cherry tomatoes, chopped
225 g / 8 oz / 1 ½ cups raw prawns (shrimps), peeled
75 g / 2 ½ oz / ½ cup feta cheese, crumbled
2 tbsp flat leaf parsley, chopped

1. Sprinkle the onion in an even layer in the base of a slow cooker and pour over the wine. Arrange the peppers on top, cut side up, and fill with tomatoes, prawns, feta and parsley. Season with salt and pepper.
2. Cover and cook on medium for 2 hours or until the peppers are tender.

Raised Pork Pie

50 g / 1 ¾ oz / ¼ cup reduced fat
  baking spread
200 g / 7 oz / 1 ⅓ cups plain
  (all-purpose) flour
50 g / 1 ¾ oz / ⅓ cup strong white bread flour
50 g / 1 ¾ oz / ¼ cup lard
200 g / 7 oz / 1 ⅓ cups lean minced pork
200 g / 7 oz / 1 ⅓ cups pork loin,
  finely chopped
100 g / 3 ½ oz / ⅔ cup smoked streaky
  bacon, finely chopped
1 onion, finely grated
1 tsp fresh sage, finely chopped
½ tsp white peppercorns, freshly ground
½ tsp nutmeg, freshly grated

1. Rub the butter into the two flours with 1 teaspoon of salt until the mixture
   resembles fine breadcrumbs.
2. Put the lard in a saucepan with 100 ml water and bring to the boil, then stir it into
   the flour.
3. Turn out the dough and knead for 1 minute or until smooth. Reserve a quarter of
   the dough for making the lid then roll the rest out into a large circle and use it to
   line the base and 10 cm (4 in) up the sides of a small slow cooker.
4. Mix the rest of the ingredients together and season with salt. Pack the mixture
   into the pastry case and brush round the outside with water. Roll out the reserved
   pastry for the lid and crimp the edges. Trim away any excess pastry and slash a
   hole in the top for the steam to escape.
5. Chill the slow cooker insert for 30 minutes to firm up the pastry, then reassemble
   and cook on high for 1 hour 30 minutes.
6. Reduce the temperature to low and cook for 5 hours or until an internal temperature
   probe reads 72°C (160F). Leave to cool completely before cutting and serving.

Toad in the Hole

2 tbsp cold pressed rapeseed oil
4 large good quality sausages
100 g / 3 ½ oz / ⅔ cup plain
  (all purpose) flour
2 large eggs
175 ml / 6 fl. oz / ⅔ cup skimmed milk
1 tbsp parsley, chopped

1. Heat 1 ½ tablespoons of oil in the slow cooker on high for 30 minutes. Swirl to coat
   the base and 5 cm (2 in) up the sides.
2. Heat the rest of the oil in a frying pan and brown the sausages all over.
3. Put the flour in a large jug with a pinch of salt, then whisk in the eggs and milk.
   Season with salt and pepper.
4. Take the lid off the slow cooker and immediately pour in the batter. Space out the
   sausages, then put the lid back on as soon as possible.
5. Cook on high for 1 hour or until well risen. The batter should be fully cooked round
   the edges and still just a little squidgy beneath the sausages.
6. Sprinkle with parsley and serve immediately.

Quiche Lorraine

110 g / 4 oz / ½ cup reduced fat baking spread, cubed and chilled
225 g / 8 oz / 1 ½ cups plain (all-purpose) flour
2 tbsp olive oil
1 leek, finely chopped
6 rashers streaky bacon, chopped
2 cloves of garlic, finely chopped
4 large eggs, beaten
225 ml / 8 fl. oz / ¾ cup skimmed milk
75 g / 2 ½ oz / ½ cup reduced fat cheese, grated
¼ tsp nutmeg, freshly grated

1. To make the pastry, rub the baking spread into the flour until the mixture resembles fine breadcrumbs. Stir in just enough cold water to bring the pastry together into a pliable dough, then chill for 30 minutes.
2. Roll out the pastry and use it to line a round flan dish that will fit inside your slow cooker. Cover and cook on high for 2 hours.
3. Heat the oil in a large sauté pan and sauté the leek and bacon for 8 minutes. Add the garlic and cook for 2 minutes, then set aside.
4. Whisk the eggs with the milk then stir in the bacon mixture and cheese. Season generously with salt, pepper and nutmeg.
5. Pour the filling into the pastry case, then cover and cook on low for 1 hour 30 minutes or until the quiche is set in the centre.
6. For a golden finish, colour the top under a hot grill for a few minutes.

SERVES: 8 | PREP TIME: 12 MINS | MARINATE: 12 HOURS | COOKING TIME: 10 HOURS

Pulled Pork

1.8 kg / 4 lb pork shoulder joint, from the collar end

2 tbsp barbecue seasoning mix

2 tbsp olive oil

250 ml / 9 fl. oz / 1 cup chicken stock

salad and sauerkraut, to serve

1. Rub the pork all over with the barbecue seasoning, then leave to marinate in the fridge overnight.
2. Heat the oil in a frying pan and sear the pork all over until nicely coloured.
3. Transfer the pork to a slow cooker and pour in the stock.
4. Cover and cook on low for 10 hours.
5. Shred the pork into the stock with two forks and serve with salad and sauerkraut.

Pulled Lamb Burgers

1 tsp ground fennel seeds
1 tsp dried oregano
1 tsp dried mint
1 tsp ground cumin
3 cloves of garlic, crushed
2 tbsp soft brown sugar
2 tbsp smoked sea salt
1.8 kg / 4 lb boneless lamb shoulder joint
2 tbsp olive oil
250 ml / 9 fl. oz / 1 cup beef stock
8 burgers buns, halved horizontally
salad, coleslaw and garlic mayonnaise
  to serve

1. Mix the fennel, oregano, mint, cumin and garlic with the sugar and salt. Rub the mixture all over the lamb, then leave to marinate in the fridge overnight.
2. Heat the oil in a frying pan and sear the lamb all over until nicely coloured.
3. Transfer the lamb to a slow cooker and pour in the stock. Cover and cook on low for 10 hours.
4. Shred the lamb into the stock with two forks and serve in burger buns with plenty of salad, coleslaw and garlic mayonnaise.

Chickpeas with Merguez

200 g / 7 oz / 1 ⅓ cups dried chickpeas,
  soaked overnight
2 tbsp olive oil
12 merguez sausages
1 onion, quartered and sliced
2 red peppers, halved and sliced
2 cloves of garlic, sliced
2 tbsp flat leaf parsley, chopped

1. Drain the chickpeas of their soaking water, then tip them into a saucepan, cover with cold water and bring to the boil. Cook for 10 minutes then drain well.
2. Transfer the chickpeas to a slow cooker and add enough cold water to cover them by 5 cm (2 in).
3. Cover and cook on high for 4 hours or until the chickpeas are tender.
4. Towards the end of the cooking time, heat the oil in a frying pan and colour the merguez all over. Transfer to a chopping board and cut into short lengths.
5. Add the onions and peppers to the frying pan and cook over a low heat for 15 minutes, stirring occasionally. Add the garlic and cook for another 5 minutes.
6. Drain the chickpeas of their cooking liquor, reserving 350 ml. Return the chickpeas to the slow cooker and add the merguez, reserved cooking liquor and the contents of the frying pan.
7. Cover and cook on low for 30 minutes, then stir in the parsley and serve.

SERVES: 8 | PREP TIME: 15 MINS | MARINATE: 12 HOURS | COOKING TIME: 8 HOURS

Roast Lamb Shoulder

2 mild red chillies (chilies), chopped
3 cloves of garlic, chopped
6 sundried tomatoes in oil
1 tbsp fresh rosemary, chopped
1 tsp fennel seeds, crushed
1.8 kg / 4 lb boneless lamb shoulder joint
2 tbsp olive oil
250 ml / 9 fl. oz / 1 cup dry white wine

1. Put the chillies, garlic, tomatoes, rosemary and fennel in a mini food processor with a pinch of salt and pepper and blend to a paste. Alternatively, use a pestle and mortar. Rub the mixture all over the lamb, then leave to marinate in the fridge overnight.

2. Heat the oil in a frying pan and sear the lamb all over until nicely coloured.

3. Transfer the lamb to a slow cooker and pour in the wine. Cover and cook on low for 8 hours.

4. Transfer the lamb to a carving board, cover with a double layer of foil and leave to rest for 15 minutes. Carve into thick slices and serve.

Spicy Pulled Turkey

4 skinless turkey thighs, on the bone
2 tbsp barbecue seasoning mix
1 tbsp smoked paprika
2 tbsp olive oil
250 ml / 9 fl. oz / 1 cup chicken stock
2 red chillies (chilies), sliced
potato wedges, to serve

1. Rub the turkey all over with the barbecue seasoning and paprika, then leave to marinate in the fridge overnight.
2. Heat the oil in a frying pan and sear the turkey thighs all over until nicely coloured.
3. Transfer the turkey to a slow cooker and pour in the stock. Cover and cook on low for 6 hours.
4. Shred the turkey into the stock with two forks and sprinkle with chillies.
5. Serve with potato wedges.

Lamb and Red Pepper Stew

450 g / 1 lb / 2 cups lamb shoulder, cubed
2 tbsp olive oil
1 onion, finely chopped
3 red romano peppers, sliced
2 cloves of garlic, finely chopped
2 tsp fresh root ginger, finely chopped
2 red chillies (chilies), chopped
1 tsp paprika
1 tsp ground cumin
2 tbsp tomato puree
600 ml / 1 pint / 2 ½ cups lamb or
 vegetable stock

1. Season the lamb all over with salt and pepper. Heat the oil in a frying pan and sear the lamb on all sides, then transfer the pieces to a slow cooker.
2. Fry the onion and peppers in the frying pan for 5 minutes, then stir in the garlic, ginger and chillies and fry for another 5 minutes. Scrape the mixture into the slow cooker and add the spices, tomato puree and stock.
3. Cover and cook on medium for 6 hours, then adjust the seasoning with salt and pepper.
4. Ladle into warm bowls to serve.

Vegetables, Herbs and More

Rice Stuffed Squash

1 medium butternut squash, halved
   and deseeded
1 litre / 1 pint 15 fl. oz / 4 cups
   vegetable stock
2 tbsp olive oil
2 shallots, finely chopped
3 cloves of garlic, crushed
150 g / 5 ½ oz / ¾ cup risotto rice
50 g / 1 ¾ oz / ½ cup Parmesan,
   finely grated
1 small bunch parsley, finely chopped

1. Use a melon baller to gouge some of the squash flesh from the neck end, so that
   the cavity runs the whole length of the squash. Reserve the scooped out flesh and
   put the two squash halves into a snugly fitting slow cooker.
2. Heat the stock in a saucepan and keep it just below simmering point.
3. Heat the olive oil in a sauté pan and gently fry the shallots and garlic for 8 minutes
   or until golden, then stir in the rice and reserved squash flesh.
4. When it is well coated with the oil, add half of the stock and cook for 8 minutes,
   stirring occasionally. Stir in the rest of the stock and cook for 5 minutes, then stir in
   the Parmesan and parsley.
5. Fill the squash shells with the par-cooked risotto, then pour enough boiling water
   into the slow cooker to come half way up the sides of the squash.
6. Cover and cook on high for 4 hours or until a skewer slides easily into the squash.

Vegetable Rainbow Bake

2 Japanese aubergines (eggplants)
3 courgettes (zucchini)
8 tomatoes, the same diameter as the
   aubergines and courgettes
250 ml / 9 fl. oz / 1 cup dry white wine
2 cloves of garlic, finely chopped
1 tsp cumin seeds
2 tbsp olive oil
parsley, to garnish

1. Cut the aubergines, courgettes and tomatoes into 5 mm slices.
2. Pack them tightly into a slow cooker, alternating between the different
   vegetables as you go.
3. Put the wine, garlic, cumin and oil into a glass jar with a pinch of salt and pepper.
4. Screw on the lid and shake, then pour the mixture all over the vegetables.
5. Cover the slow cooker and cook on medium for 3 hours or until the vegetables
   are tender.
6. Garnish with parsley and serve immediately.

SERVES: 6 | PREP TIME: 5 MINS | COOKING TIME: 3 HOURS

Vegetable Soup with Pistou

1 butternut squash, peeled deseeded and diced
1 red pepper, deseeded and diced
¼ white cabbage, diced
125 g / 4 ½ oz / 1 cup green beans, cut into short lengths
150 g / 5 ½ oz / 1 cup baby broad beans, defrosted if frozen
2 cloves of garlic, finely chopped
600 ml / 1 pint / 2 ½ cups tomato passata
600 ml / 1 pint / 2 ½ cups vegetable stock
75 g / 2 ½ oz Parmesan, in one piece

FOR THE PISTOU
1 clove of garlic, crushed
50 g / 1 ¾ oz / 2 cups basil leaves, chopped
4 tbsp olive oil

1. Mix the vegetables with the passata and stock in a slow cooker.
2. Cover the slow cooker and cook on high for 3 hours. Taste the soup and season with salt and pepper.
3. While the soup is cooking, put the pistou ingredients in a small food processor and blitz to a runny pesto consistency.
4. Ladle the soup into six bowls and top each one with a spoonful of pistou.
5. Use a vegetable peeler to shave over the Parmesan and serve immediately.

SERVES: 4 | PREP TIME: 15 MINS | COOKING TIME: 3 HOURS

Cauliflower, Broccoli and Pasta Bake

2 tbsp reduced fat baking spread
2 tbsp plain (all-purpose) flour
600 ml / 1 pint / 2 ½ cups skimmed milk
1 tbsp Dijon mustard
100 g / 3 ½ oz / 1 cup reduced fat Cheddar, grated
½ cauliflower, broken into florets
½ broccoli, broken into florets
300 g / 10 ½ oz / 3 cups fusilli
125 g / 4 ½ oz / 1 ball light mozzarella, diced
½ tsp dried oregano
1 handful basil leaves

1. Put the baking spread, flour and milk in a saucepan. Stir over a medium heat until it bubbles and thickens, then stir in the mustard and cheddar. Season with salt and pepper to taste.
2. Toss the cauliflower, broccoli and fusilli with the sauce in a slow cooker and top with mozzarella and oregano. Cover and cook on medium for 3 hours or until the vegetables are al dente and the pasta is cooked.
3. Garnish with basil leaves and serve immediately.

SERVES: 6 | **PREP TIME: 20 MINS** | **COOKING TIME: 6 HOURS 30 MINS**

Kidney Bean and Cashew Stew

250 g / 9 oz / 1 ⅔ cups dried kidney beans, soaked overnight
250 g / 9 oz / 1 ⅔ cups cashew nuts, 150 g soaked overnight
1 onion, finely chopped
2 cloves of garlic, crushed
1 tbsp fresh root ginger, grated
400 g / 14 oz / 2 cups canned tomatoes, chopped
1 tsp ground coriander seeds
1 tsp cayenne pepper
100 g / 3 ½ oz / 3 cups baby leaf spinach
1 small bunch coriander (cilantro), chopped

1. Drain the beans from their soaking water and put them in a large saucepan of cold water. Bring to the boil and cook for 10 minutes, then drain well.
2. Meanwhile, put the 150 g of soaked cashew nuts in a food processor with 100 ml of water and blend until smooth.
3. Mix the beans with the cashew puree, onion, garlic, ginger, tomatoes, coriander and cayenne pepper, then cover and cook on medium for 6 hours. Add a little boiling water if it starts to look dry at any point.
4. Stir in the spinach, coriander and two thirds of the rest of the cashew nuts.
5. Cook for 30 minutes or until the beans are tender, but still holding their shape.
6. Season to taste with salt and pepper, then spoon into bowls and garnish with the rest of the cashews.

Pesto Pasta Bake

2 tbsp reduced fat baking spread
2 tbsp plain (all-purpose) flour
600 ml / 1 pint / 2 ½ cups skimmed milk
150 g / 5 ½ oz / ⅔ cup fresh pesto
400 g / 14 oz / 4 cups dried
  conchiglie pasta
100 g / 3 ½ oz / 1 cup reduced fat
  Cheddar, grated

1. Put the baking spread, flour and milk in a saucepan. Stir over a medium heat until it bubbles and thickens, then stir in the pesto. Season with salt and pepper to taste.
2. Tip the pasta and sauce into a small slow cooker and stir well. Cover and cook on medium for 3 hours or until the pasta is cooked.
3. Sprinkle over the cheese and cook under a hot grill for a few minutes to brown and crisp the top.

Red Pepper Risotto

2 tbsp olive oil
1 onion, finely chopped
2 red peppers, finely chopped
2 cloves of garlic, finely chopped
1 tsp smoked paprika
300 g / 10 ½ oz / 1 ½ cups risotto rice
2 medium tomatoes, finely chopped
150 ml / 5 ½ fl. oz / ⅔ cup dry white wine
750 ml / 1 pints 5 ½ fl. oz / 3 cups
  vegetable stock
50 g / 1 ¾ oz / 1 ½ cups rocket (arugula)
50 g / 1 ¾ oz / ½ cup Parmesan,
  finely grated
1 lemon, cut into wedges

1. Heat the oil in a frying pan and fry the onion and peppers over a low heat for 18 minutes. Add the garlic and paprika and stir-fry for 2 minutes.
2. Add the rice and stir over a low heat for 3 minutes to toast it, then pour in the wine and add the tomato and bubble for 2 minutes.
3. Scrape the contents of the pan into a slow cooker, add the stock and stir well. Cover and cook on high for 2 hours or until the rice is cooked.
4. Stir well and season to taste, then spoon into four warm bowls and garnish with rocket, Parmesan and lemon wedges.

SERVES: 8 | PREP TIME: 45 MINS | COOKING TIME: 3 HOURS 30 MINS

Mushroom Quiche

110 g / 4 oz / ½ cup reduced fat baking spread, cubed and chilled
225 g / 8 oz / 1 ½ cups plain (all-purpose) flour
2 tbsp olive oil
1 onion, finely chopped
200 g / 7 oz / 2 ⅔ cups button mushrooms, sliced
2 cloves of garlic, sliced
2 tbsp fresh thyme leaves, plus extra to garnish
4 large eggs, beaten
225 ml / 8 fl. oz / ¾ cup skimmed milk
75 g / 2 ½ oz / ½ cup reduced fat cheese, grated

1. To make the pastry, rub the baking spread into the flour until the mixture resembles fine breadcrumbs. Stir in just enough cold water to bring the pastry together into a pliable dough, then chill for 30 minutes.
2. Roll out the pastry and use it to line a round flan dish that will fit inside your slow cooker. Cover and cook on high for 2 hours
3. Heat the oil in a large sauté pan and sauté the onion and mushrooms for 10 minutes. Add the garlic and thyme and cook for 2 minutes, then set aside.
4. Whisk the eggs with the milk then stir in the mushroom mixture and cheese. Season generously with salt and pepper.
5. Pour the filling into the pastry case, then cover and cook on low for 1 hour 30 minutes or until the quiche is set in the centre.
6. For a golden finish, colour the top under a hot grill for a few minutes.

SERVES: **6** | PREP TIME: **16 MINS** | COOKING TIME: **7 HOURS**

Kidney Bean and Potato Curry

250 g / 9 oz / 1 ⅔ cups dried kidney beans, soaked overnight
1 onion, finely chopped
2 cloves of garlic, crushed
1 tbsp fresh root ginger, grated
1 tbsp curry powder
400 g / 14 oz / 2 cups canned tomatoes, chopped
400 g / 14 oz / 2 cups light coconut milk
2 medium potatoes, diced
2 courgettes (zucchini), halved and sliced
boiled rice, to serve

1. Drain the beans from their soaking water and put them in a large saucepan of cold water. Bring to the boil and cook for 10 minutes, then drain well.
2. Mix the beans with rest of the ingredients in a slow cooker, then cover and cook on medium for 7 hours. Add a little boiling water if it starts to look dry at any point.
3. Season to taste with salt and pepper, then serve with boiled rice.

SERVES: 4 | PREP TIME: 15 MINS | COOKING TIME: 4 HOURS

Melanzane alla Parmigiana

400 g / 14 oz / 2 cups canned
  tomatoes, chopped
1 small onion, finely chopped
2 cloves of garlic, finely chopped
1 tbsp parsley, chopped, plus extra
  to garnish
2 aubergines, sliced lengthways
250 g / 9 oz / 2 balls light
  mozzarella, grated
25 g Parmesan, finely grated

1. Mix the canned tomatoes with the
   onion, garlic and parsley and season
   with salt and pepper.
2. Layer up the tomato mixture with the
   aubergines and grated mozzarella in
   a small slow cooker.
3. Sprinkle the top with Parmesan,
   then cover and cook on medium for
   4 hours.
4. If you prefer, the top can be coloured
   under a hot grill just before serving.

MAKES: 4 | PREP TIME: 30 MINS | COOKING TIME: 3 HOURS 30 MINS

Filo Pies with Veggie Filling

½ small butternut squash, peeled deseeded and diced

1 courgette (zucchini), diced

½ tbsp fresh root ginger, grated

2 cloves of garlic, crushed

1 tsp ground cumin

1 tsp ground cinnamon

250 ml / 9 fl. oz / 1 cup vegetable stock

2 tbsp pine nuts, toasted

75 g / 2 ½ oz / ½ cup Feta cheese, diced

12 squares filo pastry

50 g / 1 ¾ oz / ¼ cup reduced fat cooking spread, melted

1. Toss the squash and courgette with the ginger, garlic, cumin and cinnamon in a small slow cooker. Pour over the stock and cook on high for 3 hours or until the vegetables are tender and the liquid has been absorbed.

2. Leave the filling to cool, then stir in the pine nuts and Feta.

3. Preheat the oven to 200°C (180°C fan) / 400F / gas 6.

4. Brush the filo squares with cooking spread and layer them up in threes. Use each set to line a hole of a large muffin tin.

5. Spoon in the filling to come level with the top of the tin, then bring the pastry sides up and scrunch to seal.

6. Bake the pies for 20 minutes or until the pastry is crisp and golden brown.

Garlic Butter Aubergines

2 aubergines (eggplants),
  halved lengthways
2 tbsp butter, softened
2 tbsp olive oil
2 tbsp flat leaf parsley, finely chopped
2 cloves of garlic, crushed

1. Score the inside of flesh of the aubergines to make a diamond pattern.
2. Beat the butter with the oil, parsley and garlic and season with salt and pepper.
3. Spread the mixture all over the cut side of the aubergines, then arrange them, cut side up in a single layer in a slow cooker.
4. Cover and cook on medium for 3 hours or until a knife slides into the thickest part of the flesh with little resistance.

Borscht

1.2 litres / 2 pints / 4 ¾ cups
  vegetable stock
450 g / 1 lb / 3 ⅔ cups beetroot, peeled
  and diced
1 bay leaf
2 tsp ground cumin
150 ml / 5 ½ fl. oz / ⅔ cup half fat
  soured cream
1 handful rocket (arugula)
breadsticks, to serve

1. Put the stock, beetroot, bay leaf and cumin in a slow cooker.
2. Cover and cook on high for 3 hours. Discard the bay leaf then ladle the soup into a liquidizer and blend until smooth with the soured cream. Season to taste with salt and pepper.
3. Serve the soup hot or chilled, with a few rocket leaves on top and some breadsticks on the side.

SERVES: **4** | PREP TIME: **20 MINS** | COOKING TIME: **2 HOURS**

Porcini Risotto

2 tbsp olive oil
225 g / 8 oz / 3 cups small porcini mushrooms, or a mixture of porcini and chestnut
mushrooms
300 g / 10 ½ oz / 1 ½ cups risotto rice
150 ml / 5 ½ fl. oz / ⅔ cup dry white wine
3 shallots, finely chopped
3 cloves of garlic, finely chopped
2 tbsp dried porcini mushrooms, soaked in boiling water for 20 minutes
750 ml / 1 pints 5 ½ fl. oz / 3 cups vegetable stock
50 g / 1 ¾ oz / ½ cup Parmesan, finely grated
2 tbsp flat leaf parsley, chopped
2 tbsp Parmesan shavings

1. Heat the oil in a sauté pan and fry the mushrooms for 8 minutes or until golden
   brown. Reserve a few whole mushrooms for the garnish and slice the rest.
   Set aside.
2. Stir the rice into the sauté pan and toast gently for 2 minutes. Add the wine and
   boil vigorously until almost completely evaporated, then scrape the mixture into a
   slow cooker.
3. Add the shallots, garlic, dried porcini and vegetable stock. Cover and cook on high
   for 2 hours or until the rice is tender.
4. Stir in the sliced mushrooms, grated Parmesan and parsley and leave to stand,
   uncovered for 5 minutes.
5. Stir well and serve, garnished with the reserved whole mushrooms and
   Parmesan shavings.

SERVES: 4 | PREP TIME: 15 MINS | COOKING TIME: 4 HOURS

Squash and Chickpea Stew

200 g / 7 oz / 1 ⅓ cups dried chickpeas, soaked overnight

2 acorn squashes, peeled, deseeded and diced (or 1 small butternut squash)

400 g / 14 oz / 2 cups canned tomatoes, chopped

50 g / 1 ¾ oz / ¼ cup mixed brown and wild rice

500 ml / 17 ½ fl. oz / 2 cups vegetable stock

1 onion, finely chopped

1 celery stick, finely chopped

2 carrots, diced

2 cloves of garlic, finely chopped

1 tsp ground cumin

1 tsp smoked paprika

chives, to garnish

1. Drain the chickpeas of their soaking water, then tip them into a saucepan, cover with cold water and bring to the boil. Cook for 10 minutes then drain well.
2. Transfer the chickpeas to a slow cooker and stir in the rest of the ingredients, except for the chives.
3. Cover and cook on high for 4 hours or until the chickpeas and squash are tender.
4. Season to taste with salt and pepper, then ladle into four warm bowls and serve garnished with chives.

Roasted New Potatoes

50 ml / 1 ¾ fl. oz / ¼ cup olive oil
3 cloves of garlic, unpeeled
2 sprigs rosemary
900 g / 2 lb small new potatoes,
  scrubbed and halved
1 small bunch dill, chopped

1. Put the oil in a slow cooker with the garlic and rosemary and heat on high for 15 minutes.
2. Stir in the potatoes and season with salt and pepper, then cook on medium for 4 hours, stirring once an hour. They are ready when a skewer slides in easily and they are starting to brown on the outside.
3. Sprinkle the potatoes with dill and serve immediately.

Baked Eggs with Peppers

2 tbsp olive oil
1 red onion, sliced
2 red peppers, sliced
2 yellow peppers, sliced
2 cloves of garlic, sliced
250 g / 9 oz / 1 ⅔ cups small
  tomatoes, quartered
1 tsp dried oregano
250 ml / 9 fl. oz / 1 cup vegetable stock
4 large eggs
a few sprigs fresh oregano

1. Put the oil in a slow cooker and heat on high. Stir in the onion and peppers and season with salt and pepper. Cover and cook for 1 hour 30 minutes, stirring every 15 minutes.
2. Stir in the garlic, tomatoes, dried oregano and stock.
3. Cover and cook on low for 2 hours. Season with salt and pepper and stir well, then break in the eggs.
4. Cover and cook for 30 minutes or until the egg whites have set.
5. Carefully spoon the eggs and peppers into four bowls and garnish with fresh oregano.

Cauliflower Curry

2 tbsp sunflower oil
1 onion, finely chopped
2 cloves of garlic, crushed
1 tbsp fresh root ginger, grated
1 tbsp curry powder
2 tbsp tomato puree
400 g / 14 oz / 2 cups canned
 tomatoes, chopped
400 g / 14 oz / 2 cups light coconut milk
1 cauliflower, broken into large florets
50 g / 1 ¾ oz / ½ cup ground almonds
150 g / 5 ½ oz / 1 cup peas, defrosted
 if frozen

1. Heat the oil in a frying pan and fry the onion, garlic and ginger over a low heat for 8 minutes. Add the curry powder and tomato puree and stir for 2 minutes.
2. Stir in 100 ml of water, then scrape everything into a slow cooker. Add the canned tomatoes and coconut milk, then stir in the cauliflower.
3. Cover and cook on medium for 3 hours. Stir in the ground almonds and peas, then cover and cook for another 30 minutes. Season to taste with salt.
4. Decant the curry into a serving bowl. To make it extra healthy, carefully remove the layer of fat that will have settled on the surface of the curry with a spoon.

Ratatouille

1 aubergine (eggplant), cubed
2 courgettes (zucchini),
 quartered and sliced
2 red peppers, deseeded and sliced
1 onion, finely chopped
2 cloves of garlic, crushed
1 tbsp fresh thyme leaves
50 ml / 1 ¾ fl. oz / ¼ cup olive oil
6 tomatoes, cut into wedges
250 ml / 9 fl. oz / 1 cup dry white wine

1. Mix all of the ingredients, except for the tomatoes and wine, in a slow cooker and season with salt and pepper.
2. Cover the slow cooker and cook on high for 2 hours, stirring every 30 minutes.
3. Add the tomatoes and wine and continue to cook for 1 hour or until the vegetables are tender.
4. Taste again for seasoning and add more salt or pepper if needed.

SERVES: 8 | PREP TIME: 45 MINS | COOKING TIME: 3 HOURS

Spinach and Feta Quiche

110 g / 4 oz / ½ cup reduced fat baking spread, cubed and chilled
225 g / 8 oz / 1 ½ cups plain (all-purpose) flour
2 tbsp olive oil
1 onion, finely chopped
2 cloves of garlic, finely chopped
150 g / 5 ½ oz / 4 ½ cups spinach, washed
4 large eggs, beaten
225 ml / 8 fl. oz / ¾ cup skimmed milk
150 g / 5 ½ oz / 1 cup feta, diced

1. Rub the baking spread into the flour until the mixture resembles fine breadcrumbs. Stir in just enough cold water to bring the pastry together into a pliable dough, then chill for 30 minutes.

2. Roll out the pastry and use it to line a round cake tin that will fit inside your slow cooker. Cover and cook on high for 1 hour 30 minutes.

3. Heat the oil in a large sauté pan and fry the onion for 8 minutes. Add the garlic and cook for 2 minutes. Pack as much spinach into the pan as you can and put on the lid.

4. Cook for 2 minutes, then stir well and add more spinach. Continue until all the spinach is well wilted, then tip it into a sieve and squeeze out as much liquid as possible.

5. Whisk the eggs with the milk then stir in the spinach mixture and feta. Season with salt and pepper.

6. Pour the filling into the pastry case, then cover and cook on low for 1 hour 30 minutes or until the quiche is set in the centre.

SERVES: **4** | PREP TIME: **20 MINS** | COOKING TIME: **2 HOURS**

Squash Risotto

1 small crown prince squash, peeled, deseeded and diced
300 g / 10 ½ oz / 1 ½ cups risotto rice
150 ml / 5 ½ fl. oz / ⅔ cup dry white wine
2 shallots, finely chopped
2 cloves of garlic, finely chopped
750 ml / 1 pints 5 ½ fl. oz / 3 cups vegetable stock
¼ tsp nutmeg, freshly ground
50 g / 1 ¾ oz / ½ cup Parmesan, finely grated

1. Mix all of the ingredients together in a slow cooker, except for the Parmesan.
   Cover and cook on high for 2 hours or until the rice and squash are both tender.
2. Stir in the Parmesan and leave to stand, uncovered for 5 minutes.
3. Stir well then spoon into four warm bowls and serve immediately.

Broccoli Quiche

110 g / 4 oz / ½ cup reduced fat baking
 spread, cubed and chilled
225 g / 8 oz / 1 ½ cups plain
 (all-purpose) flour
2 tbsp olive oil
1 large leek, sliced
1 small head broccoli, broken into florets
2 cloves of garlic, sliced
100 g / 3 ½ oz / ½ cup roasted red
 peppers, drained and chopped
4 large eggs, beaten
225 ml / 8 fl. oz / ¾ cup skimmed milk
75 g / 2 ½ oz / ½ cup reduced fat
 cheese, grated

1. To make the pastry, rub the baking spread into the flour until the mixture resembles
   fine breadcrumbs. Stir in just enough cold water to bring the pastry together into a
   pliable dough, then chill for 30 minutes.
2. Roll out the pastry and use it to line the base and 6 cm (2 ½ in) up the sides of a
   small round slow cooker. Cover and cook on high for 1 hour 30 minutes.
3. Heat the oil in a large sauté pan and sauté the leeks and broccoli for 10 minutes.
   Add the garlic and cook for 2 minutes, then set aside.
4. Whisk the eggs with the milk then stir in the broccoli mixture. Season generously
   with salt and pepper.
5. Pour the filling into the pastry case and scatter the cheese on top.
6. Cover and cook on low for 1 hour 30 minutes or until the quiche is set in the centre.

Cauliflower Cheese

2 tbsp reduced fat cooking spread
2 tbsp plain (all-purpose) flour
600 ml / 1 pint / 2 ½ cups skimmed milk
1 tbsp Dijon mustard
1 tsp paprika
150 g / 5 ½ oz / 1 ½ cups reduced fat
 Cheddar, grated
1 large cauliflower, broken into florets
1 tbsp basil, finely chopped

1. Put the cooking spread, flour and milk in a saucepan set over a medium heat.
   Stir until the sauce thickens and starts to bubble. Take the pan off the heat and stir
   in the mustard, paprika and half the cheese.
2. Arrange the cauliflower in a slow cooker then pour over the sauce.
3. Cook on medium for 3 hours or until the cauliflower is al dente.
4. Sprinkle the rest of the cheese on top and colour it under a hot grill before serving,
   sprinkled with basil.

SERVES: 8 | PREP TIME: 15 MINS | COOKING TIME: 4 HOURS

Stuffing

50 ml / 1 ¾ fl. oz / ¼ cup olive oil

2 onions, finely chopped

1 stick celery, finely chopped

2 cloves of garlic, finely chopped

1 handful sage leaves, chopped

1 tbsp rosemary, finely chopped, plus extra to garnish

300 g / 10 ½ oz / 4 cups fresh white breadcrumbs

6 slices two day old sourdough, crusts removed and cubed

2 large eggs, beaten

350 ml / 12 fl. oz / 1 ½ cups vegetable stock

low calorie cooking spray

1. Heat the oil in a sauté pan and fry the onion and celery over a medium heat for 10 minutes. Add the garlic, sage and rosemary and cook for 2 minutes.

2. Take the pan off the heat and stir in the breadcrumbs and sourdough cubes.

3. Whisk the egg into the stock, then stir it into the stuffing and season with salt and pepper.

4. Spray the slow cooker with low calorie cooking spray, then scrape in the stuffing. Cover and cook on low for 4 hours.

5. Spoon the stuffing into a serving dish and garnish with rosemary.

6. Delicious served with a roast dinner.

SERVES: **4** | PREP TIME: **10 MINS** | COOKING TIME: **4 HOURS**

Wild Rice and Courgette Pilaf

2 tbsp olive oil

6 spring onions (scallions), chopped, green and white parts separated

2 cloves of garlic, finely chopped

450 g / 1 lb / 2 ¼ cups mixed brown and wild rice

750 ml / 1 pint 5 ½ fl. oz / 3 cups vegetable stock

1 tsp ground cumin

1 tsp ground coriander

2 courgettes (zucchini), sliced

125 g / 4 ½ oz / 1 ball light mozzarella, grated

1. Heat the oil in a frying pan and stir-fry the spring onion whites and garlic for 5 minutes. Add the rice and stir for 2 minutes to toast, then scrape it into a slow cooker.

2. Stir in the stock, spices and courgette, then cover and cook on high for 4 hours or until the rice is tender.

3. Season to taste with salt and pepper, then spoon into four heatproof bowls. Sprinkle over the mozzarella and toast under a hot grill for a few minutes to melt.

4. Garnish with spring onion greens and serve immediately.

Pear and Stilton Quiches

250 g / 9 oz puff pastry
3 large eggs
200 ml / 7 fl. oz / ¾ cup skimmed milk
100 g / 3 ½ oz / 1 cup stilton, diced
1 pear, cut into 4 thick slices

1. Roll out the pastry and use it to line four mini casserole dishes which will fit inside your slow cooker in an even layer.
2. Gently whisk the eggs with the milk until smoothly combined then stir in the stilton and season with black pepper. Pour the mixture into the pastry cases and stand a pear slice up in each one.
3. Transfer the dishes to the slow cooker. Cover the slow cooker with a clean tea towel, then put on the lid and cook on high for 3 hours.
4. The quiches can be finished in a hot oven to crisp the pastry and brown the tops if you prefer.

Baked Artichokes

4 globe artichokes, trimmed and chokes removed
1 lemon, juiced
4 cloves of garlic, peeled
50 ml / 1 ¾ fl. oz / ¼ cup olive oil

1. Sprinkle the artichokes inside and out with lemon juice and season with salt and pepper.
2. Sit each artichoke on a large square of foil and push a garlic clove into each one. Drizzle with oil, then enclose each artichoke in the foil and scrunch to secure.
3. Arrange the artichokes in a snug single layer in a slow cooker and pour 2.5 cm (1 in) boiling water into the bottom. Cover and cook on high for 3 hours
4. Carefully unwrap the artichokes and check that they are tender before serving.

Beef and Vegetable Stew

450 g / 1 lb / 3 cups beef shin, cut into
  large chunks
2 tbsp plain (all-purpose) flour
2 tbsp olive oil
4 large shallots, halved
2 medium carrots, cut into chunks
8 new potatoes, peeled and quartered
2 cloves of garlic, sliced
150 ml / 5 ½ fl. oz / ⅔ cup red wine
750 ml / 1 pint 5 ½ fl. oz / 3 cups
  beef stock
2 bay leaves

1. Season the beef with salt and pepper and dust the pieces with flour to coat.
   Heat the oil in a large frying pan and sear the beef in batches on all sides.
2. Transfer the beef to a slow cooker and add the rest of the ingredients.
3. Cover and cook on low for 6 hours, stirring every 2 hours. Season to taste with
   salt and pepper before serving.

Asian Braised Beef

2 tbsp sunflower oil
450 g / 1 lb / 3 cups chuck steak, cut into
  large chunks
30 g / 1 oz piece of fresh root ginger, sliced
4 spring onions (scallions), green part
  sliced, the rest bruised
1 bulb of garlic, halved horizontally
1 small bunch coriander (cilantro), leaves
  separated from stems
2 kaffir lime leaves
75 ml / 2 ½ fl. oz / ⅓ cup shaoxing rice wine
75 ml / 2 ½ fl. oz / ⅓ cup light soy sauce
300 g / 10 ½ oz thin egg noodles
½ Chinese cabbage, quartered
150 g / 5 ½ oz / 2 cups shimeji mushrooms
2 hot red chillies (chilies), sliced
1 lime, cut into wedges

1. Heat the oil in a frying pan and sear the beef on all sides. Transfer the beef to a
   slow cooker and add the ginger, bruised spring onion whites, garlic, coriander
   stems, lime leaves, rice wine and soy sauce.
2. Add enough cold water to cover the beef, then cover and cook on low for 6 hours.
3. Cook the noodles according to the packet instructions and drain well. Divide
   between four bowls.
4. Poach the cabbage and mushrooms in 2 ladles of the beef cooking liquor for
   3 minutes, then divide between the bowls.
5. Ladle in the beef and cooking liquor and garnish with coriander leaves,
   spring onion greens and chillies. Serve with lime wedges for squeezing over.

SERVES: **6** | PREP TIME: **10 MINS** | COOKING TIME: **3 HOURS**

Braised Red Lentils

2 tbsp olive oil
1 onion, finely chopped
2 cloves of garlic, crushed
1 tsp smoked paprika
½ tsp ground cumin
1 tbsp tomato puree
1.2 litres / 2 pint / 5 cups vegetable stock
400 g / 14 oz / 3 ¼ cups red lentils
1 small bunch coriander
   (cilantro), chopped

1. Heat the oil in a frying pan and fry the onion gently for 6 minutes.
2. Add the garlic and cook for 2 minutes, then stir in the spices and tomato puree. Stir over a low heat for 2 minutes, then deglaze with a splash of the vegetable stock.
3. Transfer to a slow cooker and stir in the lentils and ½ teaspoon of salt.
4. Cover and cook on high for 3 hours or until the lentils are tender, but still holding their shape.
5. Taste and adjust the seasoning with salt and pepper, then stir in the coriander and serve.

Soups

SERVES: 6 | **PREP TIME: 10 MINS** | **COOKING TIME: 3 HOURS 30 MINS**

Tomato Soup

2 tbsp olive oil

1 onion, finely chopped

2 cloves of garlic, crushed

1 tbsp fresh thyme leaves, plus extra to garnish

1 tbsp concentrated tomato puree

400 g / 14 oz / 2 cups ripe tomatoes, chopped

1 litre / 1 pint 15 fl. oz / 4 cups vegetable stock

2 tbsp flat leaf parsley, chopped

75 ml / 2 ½ fl. oz / ⅓ cup 0 per cent fat Greek yogurt

1. Heat the oil in a slow cooker set to high. Still in the onion, garlic and thyme, then season with salt and pepper. Cover and cook for 30 minutes, stirring every 10 minutes.

2. Stir in the tomato puree, tomatoes and stock, then cover and cook on low for 3 hours.

3. Transfer the soup to a liquidizer with the parsley and blend until smooth, then pass the soup through a sieve to remove any seeds and bits of skin.

4. Taste for seasoning then ladle the soup into warm bowls or mugs. Stir a little yogurt into each one and garnish with thyme and black pepper.

SERVES: **4** | PREP TIME: **10 MINS** | COOKING TIME: **2 HOURS**

Asparagus Soup

450 g / 1 lb asparagus spears, halved and woody ends snapped off
1 leek, finely chopped
2 cloves of garlic, crushed
1 litre / 1 pint 15 fl. oz / 4 cups vegetable stock
150 ml / 5 ½ fl. oz / ⅔ cup 0 per cent fat Greek yogurt
croutons, to serve

1. Put the asparagus, leek and garlic in a slow cooker and pour over the stock.
2. Cover the slow cooker and cook on low for 2 hours.
3. Transfer a few asparagus tips to a plate and reserve for the garnish.
4. Transfer the soup to a liquidizer and add the yogurt, then blend until smooth.
5. Season to taste with salt and pepper, then ladle into warm bowls and serve garnished with croutons and the reserved asparagus tips.

SERVES: 4 | PREP TIME: 15 MINS | COOKING TIME: 7 HOURS 15 MINS

French Onion Soup

2 tbsp olive oil
3 onions, quartered and sliced
1 tbsp fresh thyme leaves
2 bay leaves
2 cloves of garlic, sliced
1 tbsp balsamic vinegar
1 tbsp runny honey
1 tbsp plain (all-purpose) flour
125 ml/ 4 ½ fl. oz / ½ cup dark ale
1 litre / 1 pint 15 fl. oz / 4 cups vegetable stock
1 baguette, sliced
150 g / 5 ½ oz / 1 ½ cups reduced fat cheese, grated

1. Heat the oil in a slow cooker on high for 15 minutes. Stir in the onions, thyme, bay leaves, garlic, balsamic and honey and season well with salt and pepper.
2. Cover and cook on high for 1 hour, stirring every 15 minutes.
3. Stir in the flour, then gradually incorporate the ale and stock, stirring as you go to eliminate any lumps. Cover and cook on low for 6 hours.
4. Taste the soup for seasoning and adjust with salt and pepper, then ladle into bowls.
5. Top the bowls with slices of baguette and sprinkle with cheese, then cook under a hot grill until the cheese has melted and browned.

SERVES: 4 | PREP TIME: 10 MINS | COOKING TIME: 3 HOURS

Mushroom and Basil Soup

1 leek, finely chopped

2 cloves of garlic, crushed

300 g / 10 ½ oz / 4 cups mushrooms, sliced

1 litre / 1 pint 15 fl. oz / 4 cups vegetable stock

100 ml / 3 ½ fl. oz / ½ cup 0 per cent fat Greek yogurt

1 bunch basil, stems removed

1 small bunch chervil, stems removed

croutons, to serve

1. Put the leek, garlic and mushrooms in a slow cooker and pour over the stock.
2. Cover the slow cooker and cook on low for 3 hours.
3. Transfer the soup to a liquidizer and add the yogurt, basil and half the chervil. Blend until smooth.
4. Season to taste with salt and pepper, then ladle into warm bowls and serve garnished with croutons and chervil.

SERVES: 6 | **PREP TIME: 10 MINS** | **COOKING TIME: 4 HOURS**

Pumpkin Soup

600 g / 1 lb 5 ½ oz / 3 cups pumpkin or butternut squash, peeled, deseeded and cut into chunks

1 onion, finely chopped

2 cloves of garlic, finely chopped

1 tbsp fresh thyme, leaves only

1 litre / 1 pint 15 fl. oz / 4 cups vegetable stock

75 ml / 2 ½ fl. oz / ⅓ cup 0 per cent fat Greek yogurt

2 tbsp pumpkin seeds

1. Mix the pumpkin with the onion, garlic and thyme in a slow cooker, then pour over the stock and season well with salt and pepper.

2. Cover the slow cooker and cook on high for 4 hours.

3. Transfer the soup to a liquidizer and blend until smooth. Taste the soup and adjust the seasoning.

4. Pour the soup into warm bowls and top each one with a dollop of yogurt and a sprinkle of seeds.

SERVES: **4** | PREP TIME: **15 MINS** | COOKING TIME: **3 HOURS**

Cauliflower Soup

1.2 litres / 2 pints / 4 ¾ cups vegetable stock
1 large cauliflower, chopped
1 large potato, peeled and diced
1 bay leaf
150 ml / 5 ½ fl. oz / ⅔ cup 0 per cent fat Greek yogurt
50 g / 1 ¾ oz / ½ cup Parmesan, finely grated
¼ tsp nutmeg, freshly grated

1. Put the stock, cauliflower, potato and bay leaf in a slow cooker.
2. Cover and cook on low for 3 hours. Discard the bay leaf and reserve a few pieces of cauliflower for a garnish.
3. Ladle the soup into a liquidizer and add the yogurt, Parmesan and nutmeg. Blend until smooth, then season to taste with salt and pepper.
4. Pour the soup into four warm bowls and garnish with the reserved cauliflower and a good grind of black pepper.

SERVES: **6** | PREP TIME: **20 MINS** | COOKING TIME: **4 HOURS**

Pork, Kale and Potato Soup

2 tbsp olive oil
1 onion, finely chopped
2 cloves of garlic, finely chopped
1 tsp fennel seeds, crushed
4 good quality pork sausages, skinned
4 rashers smoked streaky bacon, chopped
3 medium potatoes, cubed
1 litre / 1 pint 15 fl. oz / 4 cups vegetable stock
150 g / 5 ½ oz / 4 ½ cups curly kale, stems removed and torn into bite sized pieces
150 ml / 5 ½ fl. oz / ⅔ cup low fat natural yogurt

1. Heat the oil in a frying pan and fry the onion over a low heat for 10 minutes.
   Increase the heat to medium and add the garlic, fennel, sausage and bacon.
   Stir-fry for 5 minutes or until the sausagemeat colours a little.
2. Scrape everything into a slow cooker and add the potatoes and stock.
3. Cover the slow cooker and cook on high for 4 hours. Add the kale halfway through.
4. Turn off the slow cooker and remove the inner cooking pot. Stir in the yogurt,
   then season to taste with salt and pepper.
5. Ladle into six bowls and serve immediately.

SERVES: 4-10 | PREP TIME: 10 MINS | COOKING TIME: 4 HOURS

Carrot and Squash Soup

1 small butternut squash, peeled, deseeded and cut into chunks

2 large carrots, peeled and diced

1 onion, finely chopped

2 cloves of garlic, finely chopped

1 tsp ground coriander seeds

1 litre / 1 pint 15 fl. oz / 4 cups vegetable stock

150 ml / 5 ½ fl. oz / ⅔ cup 0 per cent fat Greek yogurt

2 tbsp pumpkin seeds

coriander (cilantro) leaves, to garnish

1. Mix the squash and carrot with the onion, garlic and ground coriander in a slow cooker, then pour over the stock and season with salt and pepper.

2. Cover and cook on high for 4 hours or until the vegetables are tender.

3. Transfer the soup to a liquidizer and blend until smooth. Ripple through the yogurt, then taste the soup and adjust the seasoning.

4. Serve the soup in four large bowls or ten small cups and garnish with pumpkin seeds, coriander leaves and freshly ground black pepper.

SERVES: 4 | PREP TIME: 10 MINS | COOKING TIME: 7 HOURS

Bacon, Beer and Cheese Soup

6 spring onions (scallions), finely chopped, white and green parts separated

1 carrot, finely chopped

1 stick celery, finely chopped

3 rashers smoked streaky bacon, chopped

350 ml/ 12 fl. oz / 1 ½ cup beer

1 litre / 1 pint 15 fl. oz / 4 cups chicken stock

30 g / 1 oz / ¼ cup cornflour (corn starch)

125 ml / 4 ½ fl. oz / ½ cup low fat natural yogurt

250 g / 9 oz / 2 ½ cups reduced fat cheese, grated

1. Put the spring onion whites in a slow cooker with the carrot, celery, bacon, beer and chicken stock.

2. Cover and cook on low for 6 hours 45 minutes.

3. Whisk the cornflour into the yogurt, then stir it into the soup.

4. Reserve a handful of cheese to garnish and stir in the rest, then cover and cook for 15 minutes.

5. Taste and adjust the seasoning with salt and pepper, then ladle into bowls and garnish with the spring onion greens and the rest of the cheese.

SERVES: 4 | PREP TIME: 15 MINS | COOKING TIME: 3 HOURS

Spinach Soup

2 leeks, chopped
2 cloves of garlic, crushed
2 potatoes, peeled and diced
1 litre / 1 pint 15 fl. oz / 4 cups vegetable stock
200 g / 7 oz / 6 cups spinach, washed
¼ tsp nutmeg, freshly grated
0 per cent fat Greek yogurt, to serve

1. Put the leeks, garlic and potatoes in a slower cooker and pour over the stock.
2. Cover and cook on medium for 3 hours or until the potatoes start to break down.
3. Stir the spinach into the soup, a couple of handfuls at a time, waiting for it to wilt down before adding the next batch.
4. As soon as it has all been incorporated, transfer the soup to a liquidizer and blend until very smooth.
5. Stir in the nutmeg and season to taste with salt and pepper.
6. Serve the soup in bowls with a dollop of yogurt on the top.

Desserts

SERVES: 8 | PREP TIME: 20 MINS | COOKING TIME: 1 HOUR 30 MINS

Chocolate, Coffee and Walnut Cake

125 g / 4 ½ oz / ½ cup stevia

200 g / 7 oz / ¾ cup reduced fat baking spread

4 large eggs

1 tsp baking powder

2 tbsp cacao powder, plus extra for dusting

1 tbsp instant espresso powder

2 tbsp skimmed milk

75 g / 2 ½ oz / ½ cup dark chocolate (min. 70 per cent cocoa solids), chopped

75 g / 2 ½ oz / ⅔ cup walnuts, finely chopped

1. Grease the inside of small round slow cooker, preferably 20 cm (8 in) in diameter, and line it with greaseproof paper.
2. Put the flour, stevia, baking spread, eggs, baking powder, cacao, espresso powder and milk in a bowl and whisk with an electric whisk for 3 minutes or until well-whipped. Fold in the chocolate and walnuts.
3. Scrape the mixture into the slow cooker and cover with a clean tea towel, followed by the lid.
4. Cook on high for 1 hour 30 minutes or until a skewer inserted in the centre comes out clean.
5. Turn the cake out onto a wire rack and leave to cool completely before dusting the top with cacao.

SERVES: 8 | PREP TIME: 45 MINS | COOKING TIME: 4 HOURS

Pecan Pie

100 g / 3 ½ oz / ½ cup reduced fat baking spread, cubed and chilled
200 g / 7 oz / 1 ⅓ cups plain (all-purpose) flour
3 large egg whites
150 g / 5 ½ oz / ½ cup runny honey
30 g cornflour (cornstarch)
1 tsp vanilla extract
1 tsp ground cinnamon
½ tsp nutmeg, freshly grated
200 g / 7 oz / 1 ⅔ cups pecan halves

1. Rub the baking spread into the flour until the mixture resembles fine breadcrumbs. Stir in just enough cold water to bring the pastry together into a pliable dough, then chill for 30 minutes.
2. Roll out the pastry and use it to line a round tart tin that will fit snugly inside your slow cooker. Cover and cook on high for 1 hour.
3. Whisk the egg whites with the honey, then whisk in the cornflour, vanilla, cinnamon and nutmeg.
4. Scrape the mixture into the pastry case and top with the pecans. Cover the slow cooker with a clean tea towel, followed by the lid, and cook on low for 3 hours.
5. Leave to cool completely before cutting and serving.

Lemon Yogurt Cakes

125 ml / 4 ½ fl. oz / ½ cup sunflower oil
75 g / 2 ½ oz / ⅓ cup stevia
1 lemon, juiced and zest finely grated, plus a little extra zest to garnish
3 large eggs
125 ml / 4 ½ fl. oz / ½ cup low fat natural yogurt
150 g / 5 ½ oz / 1 cup self-raising flour
icing (confectioner's) sugar for sprinkling

1. Put a rack in the bottom of a slow cooker and add 2.5 cm (1 in) of boiling water. Grease six individual ramekins or gratin dishes.
2. Measure the oil, sugar, lemon juice and zest, eggs and yogurt into a mixing bowl and whisk together until smoothly combined. Fold in the flour.
3. Divide the mixture between the ramekins, then layer them up in the slow cooker, on racks if necessary. Cook on high for 2 hours or until a skewer inserted in the centre comes out clean.
4. Transfer the cakes to a wire rack and leave to cool a little before serving sprinkled with icing sugar and lemon zest.

SERVES: 6 | PREP TIME: 15 MINS | COOKING TIME: 2 HOURS

Strawberry, Apple and Walnut Crumble

300 g / 10 ½ oz / 2 cups
strawberries, quartered

1 large bramley apple, peeled, cored
and chopped

1 tbsp plain (all-purpose) flour

1 tsp ground cinnamon

2 tbsp stevia

100 g / 3 ½ oz / ¾ cup walnut pieces

75 g / 2 ½ oz / ⅓ cup reduced fat
baking spread

75 g / 2 ½ oz / ½ cup wholemeal flour

40 g / 1 ½ oz / ¼ cup coconut sugar

50 g / 1 ¾ oz / ½ cup rolled porridge oats

1. Mix the strawberries and apple with
   the plain flour, cinnamon and stevia in
   a slow cooker.

2. Put the walnuts in a food processor
   and blitz until coarsely ground.
   Add the baking spread, flour and
   sugar and pulse until the mixture
   resembles fine breadcrumbs.
   Stir in the oats.

3. Take a handful of the topping and
   squeeze it into a clump, then crumble
   it over the fruit. Repeat with the rest
   of the crumble mixture and level
   the surface.

4. Cover and cook on high for 2 hours.
   Serve warm.

SERVES: **12** | PREP TIME: **15 MINS** | CHILL: **30 MINS** | COOKING TIME: **4 HOURS**

Skinny Cookies

100 g / 3 ½ oz / ½ cup coconut sugar

50 g / 1 ¾ oz / ¼ cup stevia

75 g / 2 ½ oz / ⅓ cup reduced fat baking spread, softened

1 tsp vanilla extract

1 medium egg

125 g / 4 ½ oz / ¾ cup self-raising wholemeal flour

50 g / 1 ¾ oz / ⅓ cup 100 per cent cacao baking chips

1. Cream the coconut sugar and stevia with the butter and vanilla extract until pale and well whipped then beat in the egg, followed by the flour and cacao chips. Chill in the fridge for 30 minutes or until stiff enough to shape.

2. Line a large slow cooker with greaseproof paper.

3. Divide the cookie dough into twelve balls and space six of them out in the slow cooker.

4. Cover and cook on high for 2 hours or until the cookies are set, but will still take the imprint of your finger in the centre.

5. Transfer to a wire rack to cool and repeat with the rest of the cookie dough.

SERVES: 4 | PREP TIME: 15 MINS | COOKING TIME: 1 HOUR

Peach Crumbles

1 eating apple, peeled, cored and grated
50 ml / 1 ¾ fl. oz / ¼ cup coconut
    oil, melted
2 tbsp runny honey
50 g / 1 ¾ oz / ⅓ cup plain
    (all purpose) flour
25 g ground almonds
50 g / 1 ¾ oz / ½ cup rolled porridge oats
4 under-ripe peaches, halved and stoned
1 tsp ground cinnamon
mint leaves, to garnish

1. Preheat the oven to 160°C (140° fan) / 325F / gas 3.
2. Mix the grated apple with the coconut oil and honey, then stir in the flour, almonds and oats.
3. Shape the mixture into eight balls and press into the peach cavities. Arrange the peaches in a snug single layer in a baking dish and sprinkle with cinnamon.
4. Bake the peaches for 1 hour or until the crumble topping is golden and the peaches are tender to the point of a knife. Serve garnished with mint.

SERVES: 6 | PREP TIME: 25 MINS | COOKING TIME: 3 HOURS

Berry Clafoutis

low calorie baking spray
50 g / 1 ¾ oz / ⅓ cup plain
    (all purpose) flour
50 g / 1 ¾ oz / ¼ cup stevia
2 tbsp ground almonds
300 ml / 10 ½ fl. oz / 1 ¼ cups
    skimmed milk
2 large eggs
2 tbsp reduced fat baking spread, melted
150 g / 5 ½ oz / 1 cup strawberries,
    cut into quarters
150 g / 5 ½ oz / 1 cup blueberries
icing (confectioner's) sugar for dusting

1. Spray the inside of a small slow cooker with low calorie baking spray.
2. Whisk together the milk and eggs with the melted baking spread.
3. Sift the flour into a mixing bowl with a pinch of salt, then stir in the ground almonds and stevia.
4. Make a well in the middle of the dry ingredients and gradually whisk in the liquid.
5. Arrange half the strawberries and blueberries in the slow cooker then pour over the batter.
6. Cover the slow cooker with a tea towel, followed by the lid.
7. Cook on low for 3 hours.
8. Serve the clafoutis hot or cold, garnished with the rest of the berries and a sprinkle of icing sugar.

SERVES: 10 | PREP TIME: 45 MINS | COOKING TIME: 1 HOUR 30 MINS

Raspberry Sponge Cake

200 g / 7 oz / 1 ⅓ cups self-raising flour
125 g / 4 ½ oz / ½ cup stevia
200 g / 7 oz / ¾ cup reduced fat baking spread
4 large eggs
1 tsp baking powder
1 tsp vanilla extract

TO DECORATE
100 ml / 3 ½ fl. oz / ½ cup diabetic raspberry jam (jelly)
300 ml / 10 ½ fl. oz / 1 ¼ cups 0 per cent fat Greek yogurt
150 g / 5 ½ oz / 1 cup raspberries
icing (confectioner's) sugar, for dusting

1. Grease the inside of small round slow cooker, preferably 20 cm (8 in) in diameter, and line it with greaseproof paper.
2. Put all of the cake ingredients in a bowl and whisk with an electric whisk for 3 minutes or until well-whipped.
3. Scrape the mixture into the slow cooker and cover with a clean tea towel, followed by the lid. Cook on high for 1 hour 30 minutes or until a skewer inserted in the centre comes out clean. Turn the cake out onto a wire rack and leave to cool completely.
4. Cut the cake in half horizontally and transfer the base to a serving plate. Top with jam and yogurt and scatter over the berries.
5. Put the other half of the cake on top and dust lightly with icing sugar.

SERVES: **6** | PREP TIME: **20 MINS** | COOKING TIME: **2 HOURS**

Apple Sponge

200 g / 7 oz / ¾ cup caster
  (superfine) sugar
1 large egg
3 tablespoons sunflower oil
1 tsp vanilla extract
150 g / 5 ½ oz / 1 cup plain
  (all-purpose) flour
½ tsp bicarbonate of (baking) soda
½ tsp baking powder
½ tsp cinnamon
4 apples, peeled, cored and halved

1. Whisk the sugar, egg, oil and vanilla
   extract together with an electric whisk
   for 4 minutes or until thick. Stir the
   flour, raising agents and cinnamon
   together, then fold in the egg mixture.
2. Butter the inside of a small slow
   cooker and scrape in the cake
   mixture. Slice the apple halves
   without cutting all the way through,
   then press them into the top of the
   cake mix.
3. Cover the slow cooker with a clean
   tea towel, then put the lid on and
   bake on medium for 2 hours.
4. Test the cake by inserting a skewer
   into the centre – if it comes out clean,
   the cake is done. Otherwise, continue
   to cook and check again every
   15 minutes until it is ready.
5. Leave to cool completely before
   cutting and serving.

MAKES: **24** | PREP TIME: **20 MINS** | COOKING TIME: **3 HOURS**

Almond Biscotti

2 large eggs
50 g / 1 ¾ oz / ¼ cup reduced fat baking
  spread, melted
1 orange, zest finely grated
½ tsp vanilla extract
225 g / 8 oz / 1 ½ cups self-raising flour
50 g / 1 ¾ oz / ¼ cup stevia
100 g / 3 ½ oz / 1 cup whole almonds

1. Preheat a large oval slow cooker to high and line it with a sheet of greaseproof paper.
2. Beat the eggs, baking spread, orange zest and vanilla together then stir in the flour, stevia and almonds.
3. Shape the dough into two long rolls and transfer them to the slow cooker. Cover and cook for 1 hour 30 minutes, then lift out the rolls with the greaseproof paper and leave to cool for 15 minutes.
4. Cut the rolls across into 1.5 cm (½ in) slices. Spread a single layer of slices out in the slow cooker, then leave the lid slightly ajar and cook for 45 minutes or until crisp. Repeat with the rest of the slices in batches until they are all cooked.
5. Leave to cool completely before serving.

SERVES: 8 | PREP TIME: 30 MINS | COOKING TIME: 2 HOUR 30 MINS

Plum Streusel

225 g / 8 oz / 1 ½ cups self raising flour
100 g / 3 ½ oz / ½ cup reduced fat
 baking spread, cubed and chilled
50 g / 1 ¾ oz / ¼ cup stevia
1 large egg
1 tsp vanilla extract
75 ml / 2 ½ fl. oz / ⅓ cup skimmed milk
low calorie cooking spray

FOR THE TOPPING
450 g / 1 lb / 3 cups plums, peeled,
 stoned and chopped
2 tbsp stevia
1 tsp ground cinnamon
75 g / 2 ½ oz / ¾ cup rolled oats
100 g / 3 ½ oz / ¾ cup hazelnuts
50 g / 1 ¾ oz / ¼ cup coconut sugar
2 tbsp coconut oil, melted
icing (confectioner's) sugar, for dusting

1. Sieve the flour into a mixing bowl and rub in the baking spread until it resembles
   fine breadcrumbs then stir in the stevia. Lightly beat the egg with the vanilla and
   milk and stir it into the dry ingredients until just combined.
2. Grease the inside of a small slow cooker with cooking spray, then scrape in the cake
   mixture and level the surface.
3. Cover the slow cooker with a clean tea towel, then put the lid on and bake on
   medium for 1 hour 30 minutes.
4. Meanwhile, put the plums, stevia and cinnamon in a saucepan. Cook over a
   medium heat for 15 minutes or until reduced to a thick compote.
5. Put the oats, hazelnuts, coconut sugar and coconut oil in a food processor and
   pulse until finely chopped.
6. Spoon the plums on top of the cake and sprinkle over the streusel topping.
   Cover with the tea towel and lid again and cook for 1 hour. Leave to cool
   completely before dusting with icing sugar and cutting into slices.
7. Delicious served with pouring cream.

SERVES: **6** | PREP TIME: **5 MINS** | COOKING TIME: **2 HOURS**

Mulled Wine Pears

6 pears, peeled and cored
2 tbsp stevia
750 ml / 1 pint 5 ½ fl. oz / 3 cups red wine
4 dried orange slices
3 star anise
4 cloves

1. Put all of the ingredients in a small slow cooker, then cover and cook on medium for 2 hours, turning the pears half way through.
2. Serve the pears in small glass jars, warm or chilled.

SERVES: 8 | PREP TIME: 30 MINS | COOKING TIME: 3 HOURS | CHILL: 2 HOURS

Berry Cheesecake

200 g / 7 oz / 2 cups light digestive biscuits, crushed

50 g / 1 ¾ oz / ¼ cup reduced fat baking spread, melted

2 tbsp cacao powder

600 g / 1 lb 5 oz / 2 ¾ cups low fat cream cheese

150 ml / 5 fl. oz / ⅔ cup half fat soured cream

2 large eggs, plus 1 egg yolk

2 tbsp plain (all purpose) flour

50 g / 1 ¾ oz / ¼ cup stevia

300 g / 10 ½ oz / 2 cups mixed berries

mint leaves, to garnish

1. Mix the biscuit crumbs with the baking spread and cacao and press into an even layer in the bottom of a spring-form cake tin that will fit inside your slow cooker.

2. Whisk together the rest of the ingredients, except for the berries, until smooth. Fold in half of the berries, then pour the mixture into the tin and level the surface.

3. Put a rack into the bottom of your slow cooker and add 2.5 cm (1 in) of boiling water, then position the cake tin on top. Cover the top of the slow cooker with 3 layers of kitchen paper before putting on the lid.

4. Cook on high for 2 hours, then turn off the slow cooker and leave to cook in the residual heat without lifting the lid for 1 hour.

5. Take the cheesecake out of the slow cooker and leave to cool to room temperature before chilling for at least 2 hours.

6. Carefully unspring the tin and decorate the top of the cheesecake with berries and mint leaves.

SERVES: 4 | PREP TIME: 10 MINS | COOKING TIME: 3 HOURS

Sweet Potato and Marshmallow Dessert

900 g / 2 lb / 7 cups sweet potatoes, peeled and diced

1 tsp ground cinnamon

1 tsp ground ginger

¼ tsp nutmeg, freshly grated

2 tbsp stevia

2 tbsp maple syrup

50 g / 1 ¾ oz / ¼ cup reduced fat baking spread

50 g / 1 ¾ oz / ⅓ cup pecan nuts, chopped

75 g / 2 ½ oz / 1 ¼ cups mini marshmallows

1. Put the sweet potatoes in a slow cooker with the cinnamon, ginger, nutmeg, stevia, ½ a teaspoon of salt and 100 ml of water.

2. Cover and cook on high for 4 hours, stirring halfway through.

3. Add the maple syrup and baking spread and mash with a potato masher until smooth.

4. Scrape the mixture into a baking dish and top with pecan nuts and marshmallows.

5. Toast under a hot grill for a few minutes to brown before serving.

SERVES: **6** | PREP TIME: **30 MINS** | COOKING TIME: **3 HOURS** | CHILL: **4 HOURS**

Crème Brulee

600 ml / 1 pint / 2 ½ cups skimmed milk
1 vanilla pod, halved lengthways
6 large egg yolks
1 tbsp stevia
2 tbsp icing (confectioner's) sugar

1. Preheat the slow cooker to low.
2. Put the milk and vanilla pod in a small saucepan and bring slowly to a simmer.
3. Whisk the egg yolks and stevia together. Discard the vanilla pod then whisk in the hot milk. Pour the custard into 6 ramekins or bowls and cover the tops with foil.
4. Pour 2.5 cm (1 in) of water into the slow cooker, then arrange the ramekins in layers on racks.
5. Cook on low for 3 hours or until the custards are just set with a slight wobble in the centre. Remove the ramekins from the slow cooker and chill for 4 hours.
6. Sprinkle the top of the custards with icing sugar and caramelise with a blowtorch or under a hot grill. Serve immediately.

SERVES: 4 | **PREP TIME: 5 MINS** | COOKING TIME: **2 HOURS**

Poached Apples with Lingonberry Jam

4 apples, peeled, cored and halved
500 ml / 17 ½ fl. oz / 2 cups apple juice
1 star anise
1 cinnamon stick
4 cloves
100 ml / 3 ½ fl. oz / ½ cup lingonberry jam (jelly)

1. Arrange the apples cut side down in a single layer in a slow cooker, then add the juice and spices.
2. Cook on medium for 2 hours or until the apples are tender to the point of a knife.
3. Fill the cavity of each apple with jam and serve warm or chilled.

Blueberry Crumble

450 g / 1 lb / 3 cups blueberries,
plus extra to serve
1 tbsp plain (all-purpose) flour
2 tbsp stevia
75 g / 2 ½ oz / ⅓ cup reduced fat
baking spread
75 g / 2 ½ oz / ½ cup wholemeal flour
40 g / 1 ½ oz / ¼ cup coconut sugar
50 g / 1 ¾ oz / ½ cup rolled porridge oats

1. Mix the blueberries with the plain flour and stevia in a slow cooker.
2. Rub the baking spread into the wholemeal flour and stir in the sugar and oats. Take a handful of the topping and squeeze it into a clump, then crumble it over the fruit. Repeat with the rest of the crumble mixture and level the surface.
3. Cover and cook on high for 2 hours. The top can be coloured under a hot grill for a few minutes if you prefer.
4. Serve hot or cold with an extra sprinkle of fresh blueberries.

SERVES: 6 | PREP TIME: 5 MINS | COOKING TIME: 2 HOURS

Spiced Rhubarb

800 g / 1 lb 12 ½ oz forced rhubarb
2 star anise
1 cinnamon stick
1 vanilla pod, halved lengthways
3 slices fresh root ginger
50 g / 1 ¾ oz / ¼ cup stevia

1. Cut the rhubarb into short lengths and put it in a slow cooker with the spices.
2. Sprinkle over the stevia and 3 tablespoons of water, then cover and cook on medium for 2 hours.
3. Serve warm or leave to cool completely before chilling in the fridge.

SERVES: **4** | PREP TIME: **20 MINS** | COOKING TIME: **1 HOUR**

Skinny Chocolate Lava Cakes

low calorie cooking spray
2 tbsp cacao powder
100 g / 3 ½ oz / ⅔ cup dark chocolate, min. 70 per cent cocoa solids, chopped
100 g / 3 ½ oz / ½ cup reduced fat cooking spread
25 g stevia
2 large eggs, plus 2 egg yolks
1 tbsp plain (all purpose) flour

1. Put a rack inside a slow cooker and add 2.5 cm (1 in) of boiling water, then set it to high.
2. Coat the inside of four ramekins with cooking spray and dust with cacao.
3. Melt the chocolate, cooking spread and stevia together in a saucepan, stirring to dissolve the stevia. Leave to cool a little then beat in the eggs and egg yolks and fold in the flour.
4. Divide the mixture between the ramekins, then transfer them to the slow cooker. Lay 3 layers of kitchen paper over the top of the slow cooker before putting on the lid to absorb the condensed steam.
5. Cook for 1 hour on medium or until the lava cakes are set round the outside, but still molten within. Serve immediately.

SERVES: 6 | PREP TIME: 20 MINS | COOKING TIME: 3 HOURS

Bread and Butter Pudding

8 slices white bread

2 tbsp low fat spread

6 medjool dates, stoned and torn into pieces

75 g / 2 ½ oz / ⅓ cup dried cranberries

400 ml / 14 fl. oz / 1 ⅔ cups skimmed milk

3 large eggs

1 tsp ground cinnamon

2 tbsp stevia

1. Put a rack inside a slow cooker and add 2.5 cm (1 in) of boiling water, then set it to high. Grease a baking dish that will fit inside the slow cooker.

2. Spread the bread with low fat spread then tear into pieces and toss with the dates and cranberries in the baking dish.

3. Whisk the milk with the eggs, cinnamon and stevia and pour it over the bread.

4. Cover the pudding with buttered foil, then transfer the dish to the slow cooker. Cover and cook on high for 3 hours or until set with just a slight wobble in the middle.

Cranberry Crumbles

450 g / 1 lb / 3 cups cranberries, plus a few
  extra to serve
1 tbsp plain (all-purpose) flour
50 g / 1 ¾ oz / ¼ cup stevia
75 g / 2 ½ oz / ⅓ cup reduced fat
  baking spread
75 g / 2 ½ oz / ½ cup wholemeal flour
40 g coconut sugar
100 g / 3 ½ oz / 1 cup rolled porridge oats

1. Mix the cranberries with the plain flour and stevia and divide between four large mugs that will fit inside your slow cooker in a single layer.
2. Rub the baking spread into the wholemeal flour and stir in the sugar and oats. Take a handful of the topping. Squeeze it into a clump, then crumble it into the first mug. Repeat with the rest of the crumble mixture, alternating between the mugs.
3. Pour 2.5 cm (1 in) boiling water into the slow cooker and put the mugs inside. Cover and cook on high for 2 hours.
4. Serve hot or cold, topped with a few extra fresh cranberries.

Chocolate and Banana Loaf Cake

4 very ripe bananas
110 g / 4 oz / ⅔ cup coconut sugar
2 large eggs
120 ml / 4 fl. oz / ½ cup sunflower oil
225 g / 8 oz / 1 ½ cups wholemeal flour
2 tbsp cacao powder
2 tsp baking powder

1. Line a loaf tin that will fit inside your slow cooker with oiled greaseproof paper.
2. Mash three of the bananas with a fork then whisk in the sugar, eggs and oil.
3. Sieve the flour, baking powder and cacao into the bowl and stir just enough to evenly mix all the ingredients together. Slice the final banana and fold it in.
4. Spoon the mixture into the prepared tin and transfer it to the slow cooker. Cover the slow cooker with a clean tea towel, then put on the lid.
5. Cook on medium for 2 hours or until a skewer inserted into the centre of the cake comes out clean. Transfer the cake to a wire rack and leave to cool completely before cutting.

Index

Almond Biscotti 82

Apple Sponge 81

Asian Braised Beef 58

Asparagus Soup 63

Bacon, Beer and
Cheese Soup 70

Baked Artichokes 57

Baked Eggs with
Peppers 50

Beef and Vegetable
Stew 58

Beef Stroganoff 27

Berry Cheesecake 85

Berry Clafoutis 79

Blueberry Crumble 89

Borscht 47

Braised Beef with
Oyster Sauce 10

Braised Red Lentils 59

Bread and Butter
Puddings 92

Broccoli Quiche 54

Carrot and Squash
Soup 69

Cauliflower, Broccoli and
Pasta Bake 40

Cauliflower Cheese 54

Cauliflower Curry 51

Cauliflower Soup 67

Cheesy Chicken Bake 25

Chicken and
Vegetable Broth 19

Chicken Pie Filling 21

Chickpeas with
Merguez 33

Chocolate and Banana
Loaf Cake 93

Chocolate, Coffee and
Walnut Cake 74

Chorizo and
Butterbean Stew 18

Cod, Broccoli and Potato
Gratin 17

Cottage Pie 10

Cranberry Crumbles 93

Creamy Chicken
with Peas 9

Crème Brulee 87

Filo Pies with Veggie
Filling 46

French Onion Soup 64

Garlic Baked Chicken 19

Garlic Butter
Aubergines 47

Kidney Bean and
Cashew Stew 41

Kidney Bean and Potato
Curry 44

Lamb and Red Pepper
Stew 35

Lamb, Apricot and
Chickpea Tagine 23

Lamb Chops with Tomato
Sauce 20

Lamb Hotpot 21

Lemon Yogurt Cake 76

Melanzane alla
Parmigiana 45

Mini Quiches 12

Mini Toad in the Holes
with Gravy 26

Mulled Wine Pears 84

Mushroom and Basil
Soup 65

Mushroom Quiche 43

Paella 16

Peach Crumbles 79

Pear and Stilton
Quiches 57

Pecan Pie 75

Peppers Stuffed with
Prawns and Aubergines 29

Pesto Pasta Bake 42

Plum Streusel 83

Poached Apples with
Lingonberry Jam 88

Porcini Risotto 48

Pork, Kale and Potato
Soup 68

Prawn and Vegetable
Curry 25

Pulled Lamb Burgers 33

Pulled Pork 32

Pumpkin Soup 66

Quiche Lorraine 31

Ragu for Pasta 16

Raised Pork Pie 30

Raspberry Sponge Cake 80

Ratatouille 51

Red Pepper Risotto 42

Rice Stuffed Squash 38

Rich Braised Lamb
Shanks 11

Risotto Baked Pumpkins ...9

Roast Beef Rib 28

Roast Lamb Shoulder 34

Roasted New Potatoes .. 50

Sausage, Bean and
Barley 22

Sausage and Lentil
Stew 13

Sausage and Vegetable
Casserole 24

Shepherd's Pie 27

Skinny Chocolate
Lava Cakes 91

Skinny Cookies 78

Spanish Chicken Bake 15

Spiced Rhubarb 90

Spicy Pulled Turkey 35

Spinach and Feta
Quiche 52

Spinach Soup 71

Squash and Chickpea
Stew 49

Squash Risotto 53

Steak and Swede Slice 14

Strawberry, Apple and
Walnut Crumble 77

Stuffing 55

Sweet Potato and
Marshmallow Dessert .. 86

Thai Fish Soup 26

Toad in the Hole 30

Tomato Soup 62

Vegetable Rainbow
Bake 38

Vegetable Soup with
Pistou 39

Waterbath Lamb
Chops 8

Wild Rice and Courgette
Pilaf 56